The Armored Rose

the physiology and psychology of women fighting in the SCA

Duchess Elina of Beckenham

Aka Tobi Beck

Beckenham Publications

Avon, IN

978-0-9669399-0-3

© Tobi Beck, 1992

All rights reserved. No reproduction, copy or transmission of this publication may be made without written permission.

First Edition 1999

Second Publishing 2003

Electronic Publication 2011

Second Edition 2012

Dedication:

This book is dedicated to my husband, Stephan Beck, who had the wisdom to know there was a style there to develop and the patience to let it emerge.

And

This is dedicated to Sir Trude Lacklandia, Lady Mary of Uffington, and Sir Maythen Gervaise who laid the foundation for the road we now travel . . . . . and all the present and future Armored Roses who extend the road every day.

Special Thanks

Steve Beck, aka Duke Sir Stephen of Beckenham – For modeling, reading and listening and sanity when I was short.

Mari Asonte – aka Duchess Sir Mari – for modeling, reading, providing humor and helping sort out some of the fine pints.

Lisa Morgan - aka Lord Lyon – for teaching me typesetting and her encouragement.

Andra Barrow, - aka Hn Lady Grainne – For maintaining a website and mailing list where information on women fighting in the SCA is shared freely, and for being a place to vent as necessary.

Mike Canfield, - aka Viscount Sir Richard for the delightful cartoons of the 'Lizard Brain' come to life.

Kevin Griggs - aka Duke Sir Finn, and **Scott Frappier** - aka Duke Felix for never letting me fight them one inch less than I could, and enjoying it.

This book makes specific references to the Society for Creative Anachronism, (SCA), a Medieval Recreationist Organization, dedicated to the study of the Middle Ages. The fighting referenced here is based on the full contact, full speed tournament and war style marshal art practiced by this group. For more information on the SCA, see the web site: www.sca.org. Many other organizations such as martial art studios and police training academies have used these techniques and observations with great success.

Contents

Introduction vii
    by Viscountess Sir Maythen Gervaise (of Elfhaven),
    Duchess Hoghton.. vii

I. Prelude 1
    Why this Book? 3
    Historically Speaking 7

II. The Physical 15
    The Most Noticeable Differences 17
    The Hand 23
    The Arm 29
    The Hip 35
    The Hipbone is connected to the Leg Bone 43

III. Physiological 45
    Understanding Chemistry 47

IV. Psychological 55
    The Lizard Brain 57
    Hurdle One: I can play this game 61
    Hurdle Two: I can Hit 67
    Hurdle Three: I can be hit! 72
    Hurdle Four: I can't do this, yet. 77
    Hurdle Five: Fighting outside the Comfort Zone 81

  Final Note on Hurdles 84

V. Prejudices and Pondering 87

  Prejudices 89

  Choosing a Trainer 93

  Why does she fight? 96

VI. Practical 99

  Blows and Blocks 101

  Practice drills on your own 167

  Practice Drills with a Partner 172

VII. Promise 175

  My Lady Doth Carry a Big Stick 177

  The Magic Sword 184

  The Time of My Life 190

Introduction

by Viscountess Sir Maythen Gervaise (of Elfhaven), Duchess Hoghton

When Tobi (Duchess Elina) asked me to contribute to this book I jumped at the chance for a number of personal reasons. First, mundanely I have been a professional writer (among other things) for some time, but have taken a leave of absence to pursue a Ph. D., for which I am currently finishing my dissertation, and it would give me a chance to do some "real" writing. Second, because of school I have become fairly inactive in the SCA, certainly as a fighter. No time, no energy, no money! I hadn't given that much thought to the problems of fighting in the recent past until Tobi and I had a long chat at the Boar Hunt and Feast this past December and brought up this project. She sent me a follow-up email in which she said:

> I'm sure you do not remember it but we first met about 9 years ago at Estrella when I was Queen of Trimaris. You were at the Griffin's Guard camp enjoying the fire, and we fell to disagreement on some subject or another, I have no idea what. What amazed me and endeared me was that you approached the argument with dignity and poise, never taking pock shots or discounting the value of another opinion. I remember pointing out that I had done a great deal of soul searching on the subject and you said "No opinion of value comes without it". The memory and the message have served me well, and I thank you for them.

I thank her for her kind words, and I think I vaguely remember that conversation. (That is a comment on my memory, not her memorability!) I certainly can reconstruct what we said. She must have said something about women fighters being different. I said something about a fighter is a fighter is a fighter. Gender has no place on the field.

As an old codger, now I am going to give a history lesson, or at least get up on a soapbox, which I have carried around lo these many years. You have to understand that I discovered and joined the SCA in about A.S. III. Women did not fight. Women who did were ridiculed and driven out by the "old boys". Tales were told about them which were right up there with the kind of tales told about strong women ("lezzies") in high school. I quit. I had other things to do in the sixties and seventies other than put up with that kind of garbage. That garbage was not new to me, nor would it slink off and rot.

I had received a post-baccalaureate scholarship to Wood's Hole Marine Biological Laboratory and Oceanographic Institutes in the summer of 1960. I was 20, a graduate student and a blooming scholar of botanical ecology, back in the bad old days when ecology wasn't a bumper sticker. In fact nobody much knew what it was or how vital it was going to be. I had already published an undergraduate honors paper on lichens as bio-indicators of pollution, and was preparing a paper for publication in a major journal that summer. When it came my turn to go out on the boat to gather my samples, I was told that since the Navy owned the boat, no women were allowed on board. I argued my case to the Captain. I lost. A male colleague took time from his work to get my samples, but I felt cheated and ashamed. Now when I see a crew of male and female sailors and officers aboard a U.S. Navel vessel I cheer and sometimes cry.

When I was in college there was a quota on women in medical school, and no woman was allowed to train as a surgeon. No women astronauts, no women fighter pilots, no Xena's or Buffy's for role models. "Girls" didn't get to do the good stuff. There were great inequalities and many of those in my generation fought hard to be treated as equals.

Here, even in the SCA, the inequality showed on the field. When I first joined in A. S. III women weren't allowed to fight, and the few who tried (before Trudi Lacklandia paved the way, with support from Duke William of Hoghton who was then on the BOD) were not treated nicely and eventually gave up. Since fighting was the "something special" which made the SCA magical and noble and different from Faire or theatre or other activities, I left. I bumped into us again around A.S. XII, on the heels of a divorce, a single mother of three. I found old friends, made new ones, and finally began to fight, my dream of Knighthood which I had held in my heart since I was a child first reading of Arthur and his Round Table finally on the horizon.

Not that all the problems of equality were solved. Mary of Ufington had already been knighted and I met her at practice. She was the second female knight, I would be the third. She was a pretty hot fighter, but she had lost several rounds, and was heading back into the house for something. She looked pretty unhappy. Here I was, a no account unbelt, just starting out, but I said something to her which I certainly do remember, even if she doesn't. "Women are taught to compete and lose, especially in the higher social classes. It makes men feel better to compete against an almost worthy opponent, and then be guaranteed a victory. Just go out there and win." The statement was true twenty years ago. At the time, I was told and I really believed I couldn't hit hard enough.

I endured all the "test" concussions to see if I had what it took (oh, they will deny it, but it is all too true). I was the first on the field and the last off, well or ill, injured or not, because if a woman "wimped out" it was just more grist for the mill that we didn't have what it took, we didn't belong. Here I was, in my late 30s and early 40s, five feet tall, chunky, and, despite some martial arts, yoga and dance, not an athlete by my own reckoning, bound and determined to beat the boys at their own game. Oddly enough I came to dislike women. They were weak. They mostly didn't have what it took. And when they wanted to compete, they wanted to change the rules to accommodate them. I had no patience with this. I knew from experience that if us women didn't stand toe to toe with the old boys, or the young boys, we would never break the steel ceiling. And so I lost patience with women who weren't with me, because if they weren't with me they were against me, and this was war.

There were men, knights, and even dukes, who wouldn't fight me because it was unchivalrous to hit a woman. The subtext was so clear. The only way they would consider hitting a woman would be as a chattel to be punished or victim to be hurt. There were and are a lot more who won't take a blow from a woman. A certain very famous duke has said many times that a woman can't kill him because no woman CAN hit hard enough. Well, if you don't fall down even when your armor is dented and you are reeling with a headache, no you can't be killed. Ego has an infinite armor rating.

Yes, this may sound angry, but it is also true. I resolved early on that I would not compete in an all-girl tourney, or accept being the best girl on the field. I would not be "just a woman." I would be a fighter, and when that helm went on no one would know what my gender was. Just that I had won or lost honorably, and preferably won. And unlike some other women, I didn't need to wear eye shadow under my helm or at the revel. I was tough. Tough was quite sexy enough for me. I lived this chapter in our not so distant past. There is no surprise that when this young Queen came up to me saying that we were different and needed to fight differently, I saw the same weakness that I had held in contempt before.

Some things may be changing. I have been and still am an active pagan. The goddess movement has given me a theology which allows me to have self respect, as a women, not property. I'm respected today in my chosen field. I am the Doctorate Candidate that I could not be almost forty years ago. Women have spent those years, almost a lifetime, demanding equality, and in some measure it has come. In the SCA we have demanded to be treated the same. I didn't come all this way, carrying the joint and psychic damage, which I endured, to get where I got, just to give it up because women are different. The joint damage is the physical reminder but the psychic damage is there as well. No matter how many men, and there have been a lot, tell me that I killed them in this or that place and they learned so much from fighting me, somewhere inside me I still feel I am not a knight equal to my brothers and I can't teach worth beans. I know that isn't true, in daylight, but at night… There are scars. Scars I'd like to prevent in other women called to the field of honor.

Tobi has developed a new fighting style based on her SCA and military experience, which she feels, will give women a leg up. I'm willing to try it. The style is designed with the woman's body and head in mind. It's a style that examines and steers around the damage that was done when I learned. Maybe it is gender specific. Maybe we have moved to a time that we can be gender specific and still be equal. In my time we had to be the same in order to be equal. In being the same we may have forfeited some of our advantages, physically, mentally and psychically. Tobi contends that 'equal' does not mean 'the same', that if we are to be equal we must train to our natural advantages, as men already do. After all, if we, as women, are our own people, it is only fair that we call our own shots, so to speak. And any man with whom we train, if he is as noble and worthy as we are, and I believe most of my brothers are, will respect and cheer that. It is time to move on.

But I ask you not to forget the lessons of the past. We are at this spot in the journey because there were women in the past who refused to remain victims, chattel, property. It would be all too easy for the rights women have gained to be eroded, when we accept and acknowledge that we are different. Don't forget.

I. Prelude

Why this Book?

This book is for the women who want to fight and don't know why they just won't drag themselves to the field. This is for the women who fight, but find they procrastinate about putting on armor, or find any one of a hundred things more important to get done today, rather than fight. This is for women who fight who want to get better. This is for men who want to train women. This is for men who dread training another female, because they always seem to drop out. This is for men who will fight women. Whoever you are, and whatever your motivation, there is something here to benefit from. Try to keep and open mind as you go through this work. Many of the concepts will start off sounding a little strange or hard to believe, but it is my hope that once the explanation of a concept is finished, the concept will be clear and you will begin to recognize it in your own situation.

This manual is not intended to teach a female fighter how to fight, or even the trainer how to train. What this is meant to do is offer a variety of highlights to the differences between men and women in the physical, physiological, psychological and emotional areas that make us react and learn from one another. Men and women are wholly unalike, something most people over the age of five have noticed. Some of the differences are plain to see, yet many are not. Each difference, subtle and complex, emotional and physical, born with or developed, create characteristics unique to our respective genders. To insist that she learn the same way he does sells one or the other gender short, or sometimes both. Fighting and the techniques for fighting (in the SCA particularly) were developed by and for men. To teach her in the tried and true, accepted manner that works for him will only serve to handicap her. Given technique and training that adapt to the varied aspects of her gender, she will be as competent and willing a fighter as he is.

Men and women are unique to each other in such a variety of subtle ways and with such quiet nuance, that many differences are overlooked. That is until we attempt to learn physical exercises from each other. One analogy to explain the phenomenon is the idea of the fighter library: Each fighter is a book. Some books are better than others, some more complete, some are newer with less depth, some are older with multiple volumes, some highlight a particular style, some are general without specialty and so on. Each male fighter comes to the field with any number of books to read and study. One book may be easier to read than another for a specific fighter, or one may make more sense than another, in the same way that a one trainer may be easier to learn from. After they have learned from one, a fighter can move on to another book to suit their individual taste and style. The female fighter is allowed to use the same library, in fact many of those books will look quite inviting and welcoming. The words will look the same, but the language will be different. The problem arises when neither the reader/student nor the books/teachers know that the language is different. The book knows that the male students have learned this way and is therefore a good way to teach. The female reader knows that she is not stupid, and should be able to learn, but there is just a great deal of frustration in trying to understand what is being said. It would be like hearing A pink stripe on the cat would be nice," and knowing that the person asked what was for dinner. This manual is intended to be a translator, for the male books to the female students.

There are points within this book where the male readers will not understand how a female could have such a reaction. If you are a male unit, and at one of these places, turn to the nearest female unit and ask her if she feels this way. It is surprising to note how many women are wired very much the same. The intuitive reader may be able to gain a glimpse into the complex and mysterious world of female language and thought. In every example, you may be able to find a woman who does not match the trend I am describing, there are always exceptions. You are unlikely, however, to find a single female who is an exception to everything highlighted here. I did once. She was an exception to every physical trend that I ascribe to women. I was extremely confused, she had many of the emotional traits but none of the physical. This is the greatest danger and biggest fear when using random audience members to prove points through demonstration during a lecture – the person pulled from the audience to illustrate the point doesn't. After many uncomfortable minutes, her friends rescued me from my confusion by explaining that she had been a man the year before. As I said, everyone is different.

The last section of the book addresses specific training, armoring and fighting concepts When we examine style and technique in detail, understand that this is not the know all and end all reference. This is a place to start and a place to re-learn. <u>This is not the one true way, I don't believe there is only one way.</u> Try these styles, try others, use what works. Don't be afraid to use the unconventional if it is safe and effective for your body.

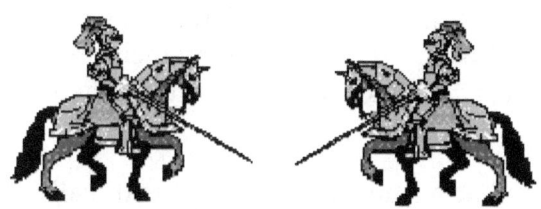

Historically Speaking

I was always taught that women did not fight, in the real world anyway. It was considered common knowledge in my military education that the only women in combat were Israeli and they were ultimately taken out of the Infantry after much debate. I knew when I entered the Army that women were not allowed in the Combat Arms (Infantry, Armor, and Air Defense Artillery) because the potential to send these troops into combat was too great. It is reasonable to be told and believe that women do not fight in combat now, and never have. Many scholars are wrapped in the same conclusion and form modern historical belief based on assumptions that current society maintains. For example we all "know" that women did not fight, so when weapons are found in *his* ancient tomb it is clear that he was a warrior, if they are in *her* tomb they are likely to be seen as symbolic of secular power. Ibn Al-Qulanisi writing first hand accounts of the first and second Crusades notes women among the armored dead, and concluded that the women were in disguise, fighting as men.[1] The conclusion is sound, based on the beginning assumption "women

---

[1] Arab Historians of the Crusades, Translated from the Arabic sources by Francesco Gabrieli, translated from the Italian by E. J. Costello, Copyright 1957 by Giulio Einaudi Editore S.p.A., Turin, Dorset Press edition 1989, ISBN 0-88029-452-3.

don't fight", which would have been true for his culture. Much of what we know of the Crusade battles comes from this and other Arabic, first hand, historian writings, but with these writings we have adopted the assumptions as well. It is easy to see where the belief of foreign historians, influenced by their own culture, writing first hand accounts could later be translated as an accurate representation of the facts.

So I was taught that women did not fight historically. I was also taught that they don't fight in the modern military either.

Then, while I was in the active Army I found myself in a combat environment, leading troops. There were no Infantry boys in the conflict at all, in fact none of the Combat Arms units were in this designated War Zone. I was a female, leading soldiers, some of them female, in combat missions, real missions, real bullets, real engagements. It was about this time that I suspected that my "knowledge" that women did not and do not enter into combat might be faulty. As I set out to research this area, I found surprising results. Women did not fight in disguise as the Arab historians, influenced by their cultural beliefs, assumed. Women fought, sanctioned by the church and the Order of Knighthood to which they belonged and with full knowledge of those around them.

Many of us know the legend of Boadicea the Queen of Celts who led an army, Artemisia, Queen of Halicarnassus, or Medb of Connacht all historical figures who have tales of mythological proportions. These should be considered along the same lines as the story of Arthur, that British King. There was probably a person the legend was based upon, sometime, in some respect, but history seems to get foggy after a few years and downright imaginative after two thousand.

Looking a little further down the path of imaginative history there was Jeanne d'Arc, who was not a noble or knight, but inspired an army. Her exploits were documented in great detail. Though recent by comparison even her story has become a little muddled since 1430. It seems that the version that the church wanted to record was different than the one bards recorded and two hundred years later there are "primary" sources that conflict with each other. Four hundred years later there is no telling what actually happened. There is significant controversy as to whether she actually fought, or just sat on a horse and acted inspirational. But she did exist. Her case is interesting to note in that her family was granted nobility, and their lands, as many, passed both through the male and female of the family.[2] Land passing through the female line seemed to be a common practice during the Middle Ages except where specifically prohibited.[3]

There are, however, many cases where women did fight, and gained the title of Knight. These cases are gained, not from the bards tale or fiction, but records and writings of the time.[4] These cases, while less famous, are not in dispute. In the High Middle Ages knighthood could be gained in three ways; holding land and supporting the local noble when called (called a knight's fee), by being inducted into an order of knighthood, which were aplenty in the Middle Ages, or by inheriting the husband's title.[5] The first two means are documentable for both men and women throughout the Middle Ages. The third, sharing the husband's title, seems to have happened only with women sharing the man's title, not vice versa.

---

[2] The original text of the Grant of Nobility survives and can be seen in its entirety at http://www.fordham.edu/halsall/french/arc.htm.

[3] After all inheriting Royal lands through the female is why Henry V went to war with France.

[4] The Military Orders from the Twelfth to the Early Fourteenth Centuries, Alan Forey, 1992. Macmillan Education LTD, Houndmill, Basingstoke, Hampshire and London, England. ISBN 0-8020-7680-7

[5] Chivalry, Leon Gautier, Translated By D.C. Dunning, J.M. Dent & Sons Ltd., Great Britain, 1965.

She would be called, *"chevaliere"*, in Medieval French when she shared the title with her husband. This was not to be confused with the word *"chevaleresses"* which was used to describe women who held fiefs and had taken the vows and accolades of knighthood. Recorded instances of the *"chevaleresses"* date between the 14th and 17th centuries. The clear usage of two different words seems to indicate that they clearly held two meanings and may have had two different statures in society. Menetrier, a 17th century scholar of chivalry wrote, "It was not always necessary to be the wife of a knight in order to take this title. Sometimes, when some male fiefs were conceded by special privilege to women, they took the rank of *Chevaleresse*, as one sees plainly in Hemricourt where women who were not wives of knights are called *Chevaleresses*."[6]

The religious Orders of knighthood such as the Templars and Hospitallers are well know to those who study the Crusades. The Arab historians Abu Ya'la Hamza ibn Asad at-Tamimi, known as Ibn Al-Qalanis, and Izz ad-Din Ibn al-Athir writing at the time even remark that women's bodies were found along with the men in the aftermath of a Crusader battle.[7] This should not be surprising when looking at the records of the Templars and Hospitallers, as by their own writings, they admitted women to the Orders.[8]

The first religious order of knighthood to grant the rank of *"militissa"* or knight, to women seems to be the Italian Order of the Glorious Saint Mary, founded by Loderigo d'Andalo in 1233. According to H.E. Cardinale in his work titled Orders of Knighthood, Awards and the Holy See, Pope Alexander IV granted this order official approval in 1261. In Military Orders in

---

[6] Orders of Knighthood, Awards and the Holy See, Edited and revised by Peter Bander Van Duren, Produced in Great Britain, Billing and Sons Limited, Worcester, 1985, ISBN 0-905715-26-8.

[7] Op. Cit. Arab Historians of the Crusades

[8] *Women and the Military Orders in the twelvth and thirteenth centuries*, Alain Forey, Studia Monastica XXIX, Montserrat, Barcelona 1987.

the Twelfth and Thirteenth Centuries, Alain Forey sites many examples of women in Military Orders. The Teutonic Order of Knighthood accepted women as *"consorores"* who wore the habit of the order and served the hospitaller functions. Buckland, England was the site of a Hospitaller Chapter house for sisters of the Order until 1540. In Aragon there were four additional Chapter houses of the Knights Hospitaller for sisters of the Order. Each of the chapter houses was headed by a *"commendatrix"*, the feminine form of the military title used for the male Chapter house equivalent. The Order of Santiago founded in 1175 established six convents for the Order by the late 13th century and these convents were headed by a *"commendadora"*. Du Cange, writing in the 17th century notes, in his work Glossarium, that the female canons of the canonical monastery of St. Gertrude in Nivelles, after a probation of three years, are made Knights. A Knight (a male called in for this purpose) gives them the accolade and performs the ceremony at the altar, complete with sword and dubbing.[9] It is unclear if these women served in both the military and hospitaller functions that the males did, but the structure and titles within the organization are identical to the male counterparts.

Religious orders were not the only places to find women given the title of Knight. Raymond Berenger, the Count of Barcelona, to honor the women who fought to defend Tortosa against a Moorish attack, founded the Order of the Hatchet (Orden de la Hacha) in Catalonia in 1149. In 1441 and 1451 orders of knighthood were founded by Catharin Baw and the House of Hornes which were open exclusively to women of noble birth. These women were given the accolade and trappings of knighthood as seen in the exclusively male orders of the day, and were granted the title of *"equitissa"* (Latin for Female Knight) or *"chevaliere"* (French for Female Knight).[10] Edmund Fellowes in his book Knights of the Garter, lists 68 women appointed to the

---

[9] Op. Cit. Orders of Knighthood, Awards and the Holy See

[10] Ibid.

Order of the Garter, between 1358 and 1488. Some of these women were neither of royal blood nor wives of other Knights of the Garter, but were appointed to this Order on their own merits, not by blood or marriage. These were addressed as "Knight of the Order of the Garter" and all wore the garter of the Order on the left arm, as did their male counterparts. Some are shown with the garter on their tombstone. [11]These women gained the title "Knight" for the same reasons and with the same obligations that male members of the order did.

As for women who fought, history, of course, tends to record by name those most notable. They were of royal lines and as a result, most of our documentable cases of women who led troops are also women who were rulers. In 900AD Aethelfled, the Queen of Mercians, led troops and fought battles in Saxon England according to the 12th Century historian William of Malmesbury. Orderic Vitalis, writing in the 11th Century of Countess Isabel in Normandy, and says she "rode armed as a knight, showing no less courage among her men-at-arms than did Camilla, heroine of Italy, among the soldiers of Tumus." According to the Greek chronicler Niketas Choniates, Eleanor of Auitaine wore "full knightly armor" and commanded forces on the field. In French history Jeanne Laisne lead the defense of the town of Beauvais in 1472 and earned herself the nickname "Hachette". While she was given the same privileges as the women of the Order of the Hatchet mentioned previously, this Order was in Spain, 323 years earlier and it is unlikely that she was inducted as a member.

There is no suggestion that it was common, Medievally for women to fight as equals on the battlefield or even lead troops, however, there are examples aplenty throughout history of women in the military arts. As for the title of "Knight", men and women both came to this accolade in the same way throughout Europe. They may have been called *"Chevaleresses"*, *"Chevaliere"*, *"Equitissa"*, *"Militissa"* or Knight depending on

---

[11] Knights of the Garter, Edmund Fellowes, Aylesbury, Bukinghamshire, England, 1939 (out of print).

the language. Italy, France, Spain, Germany, and England all had Medieval Female Knights.

It is a common belief that women did not fight and were not knights, history notes otherwise. Even today, we say that women don't enter into front line combat situations. In this regard, at least, I am 100% sure that the belief is a misconception. Share the knowledge. Once upon a time you might have made the same statement.

Update in the Second Edition: In July of 2011 the University of Western Australia published a study that indicated that women were in far greater number among the Vikings that invaded Europe than ever suspected. Previous assumptions that bands of Norse men would go Viking and raid the lands has come under suspicion because of recent DNA and osteological analysis of mass graves. Previously assumptions were made of the gender of a skeleton based on the goods buried with it.

Shane McLeod of the Centre for Medieval and Early Modern Studies did a study of 14 graves and traced the isotopes found in their bones to reveal their birthplace. Of the 14 Norse graves, six were women. The study further specifically calls out the assumption that war like materials may have initially mislead researchers about the gender of the Viking invaders – contributing to the misconception that "The Vikings" were bands of men. In a mass burial site called Repton Woods, "despite the remains of three swords being recovered from the site, all three burials that could be sexed osteologically were thought to be female, including one with a sword and shield." Ultimately the study concluded that one third to half of those Viking invaders were female.[12]

Anne Graslund also pointed out the problems of assuming gender by grave content. She also sited textual evidence of both female Viking rulers such as Thyra and Saxon text from 1200 that states

---

[12] McLeod, Shane 2011. Warriors and women: the sex ratio of Norse Migrants to eastern England up to 900 CE. *In* Early Medieval Europe 19(3).

"there were once women in Denmark who dressed themselves to look like men and spent almost every minute cultivating soldiers' skills."[13] It is my firm belief that as we put aside more assumptions, we are likely to find that warrior women have been with us all along, that it has only been through selective reasoning that we imagine they have not.

Now, let's go out and recreate history.

---

[13] Graslund, Anne Sofie 2001. The Position of Iron Age Scandinavian Women: Evidence from Graves and Rune Stones. *In* Gender and the Archaeology of Death (81-99)

II. The Physical

The Most Noticeable Differences

Let us start with something simple. Most of us have figured out that we are built differently, it's one of the things guys like about girls. The weight distribution adds up to a different center of balance between men and women of the same weight. He has a tendency to carry his weight up high in his chest, she, lower in her legs. If you balanced a man and woman on a single balance point, hers would be around the lower hip area and his in the upper waist. Her lower center of balance comes in handy when learning a martial art that involves "getting under" an opponent. In full contact "heavy" fighting this advantage is useful in moving around an opponent quickly. It is only a slight advantage, but upper level fighting is largely a matter of very small advantages that are exploited to the best ability. So, for now, stick this one in the back of the head, using it will be important when you move on to the advanced stages.

Another very obvious difference is that women have a chest that men don't. It's another one of those things that men tend to like about women. Surprisingly though, this is not a huge interference when fighting. Most women have worked around these chest protrusions since they were 12, trust that they know how to move around them. However, most men, and many women, believe that this physical difference creates vast challenges when fighting. Now let us give credit where it is due, the trainer did recognize that there was a difference and has made some attempt to address it. The female, knowing that this is a difference and trusting that her trainer knows what he is talking about, believes him. Chances are, however, that the trainer does not have these same chest protrusions for himself and is personally unaware that she has had a great deal of experience moving around hers. Further, now she has another excuse to use as to why she is not able to fight as well as others. We will review what generates most excuses in a later chapter.

What to do? Simple! Armor her as if she were a barrel-chested man and move on. If you take a cross section of a man's chest you will find that some are round, others are oblong and still others are amazingly flat. They all seem to be able to fit into body armor, and so can she. Just as that barrel-chested man can fit into body armor and move comfortably, so will she, with properly fitted body protection. As of 2011 rigid protection for the chest is NOT required. In fact separate breast cups are prohibited unless connected by or mounted on an interconnecting rigid piece. That said, it is fairly foolish not to wear chest protection. Not because it increases the changes of breast cancer (myth) or does more damage to women than men (myth), but simply because it is more protective and hurts less when doing all out one on one fighting. I can't imagine going without mine.

So, let's address properly fitted body armor. Many women make the mistake of taking the standard Coat of Plates, Brig, Globose or other rig and making the pattern in the appropriate size and -voila!- they have body armor. The most common problem with this approach is that she looses the ability to move her arms properly. The upper edge of the body armor may dig into the spot between the front of the shoulder and the body producing a very common 'armor bite'.

Figure 1

18 II. The Physical

(Figure 1) This is often where the perception that the chest is getting in the way comes from. The common solution is to cut out the armholes large enough that they do not dig into the body when the arm is moved. This is a solution, but it is a solution for the wrong problem.

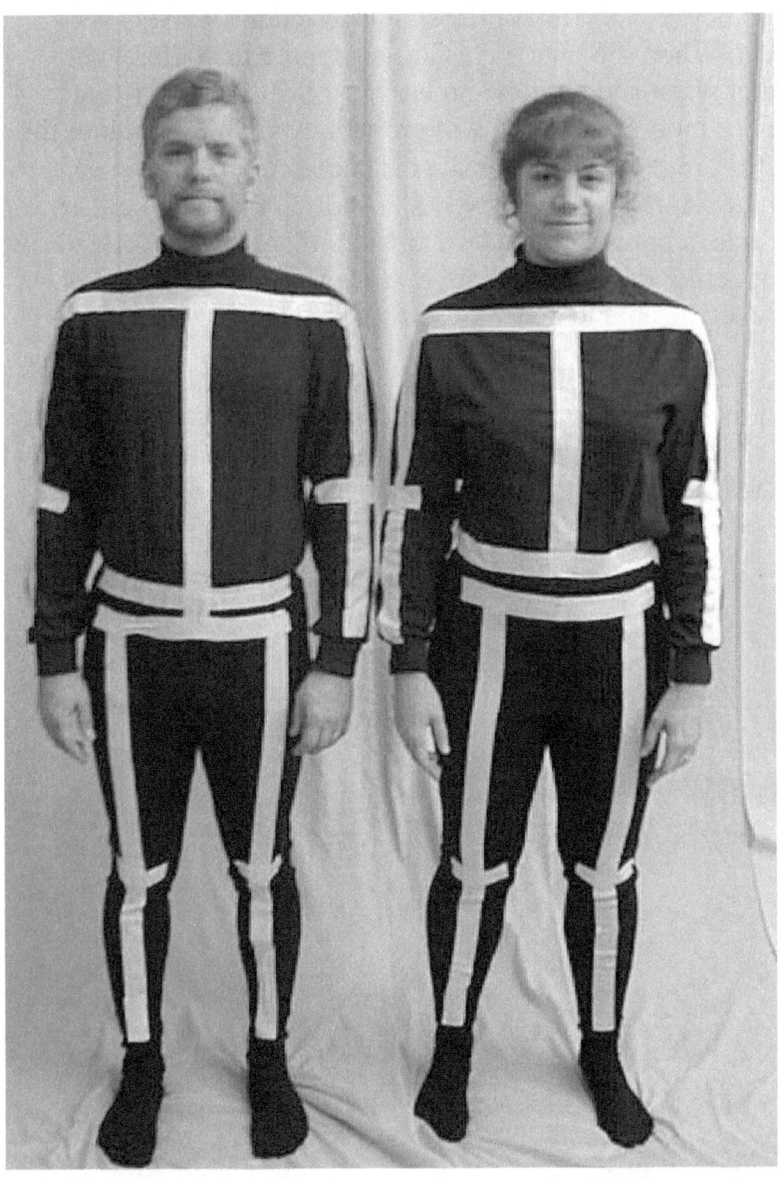

To understand the problem, we need to do a bit of comparison. The pictures show both a man and a woman of the same height, each marking knee, hip and waist. (Figure 2) Note that the natural waist on her is several inches higher than it is on him. They both have feet on the ground, they are both the same height, but the distance between the top of the shoulder and the waist is very different. When she puts on his armor it more than likely will cover her waist and go down to her hips. She will lose a huge amount of mobility and she will probably walk like a tank or the Michelin Tire Man™. The answer is not to cut off the top or widen the armholes, the answer is to shorten the length of the body. Take a note from modern fashion. If *she* tries on one of *his* shirts it comes down to mid thigh, if *he* tries on one of *hers*, he won't even be able to keep the shirt tucked in.

Look at the pictures of the man and woman again. Her waist is several inches higher, but her shoulders are at the same height as his. If she is to retain her mobility, she must have body armor that is several inches shorter in the trunk than his.

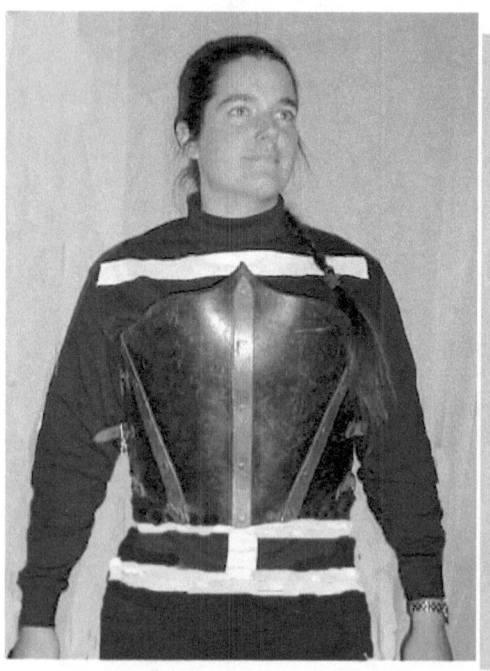
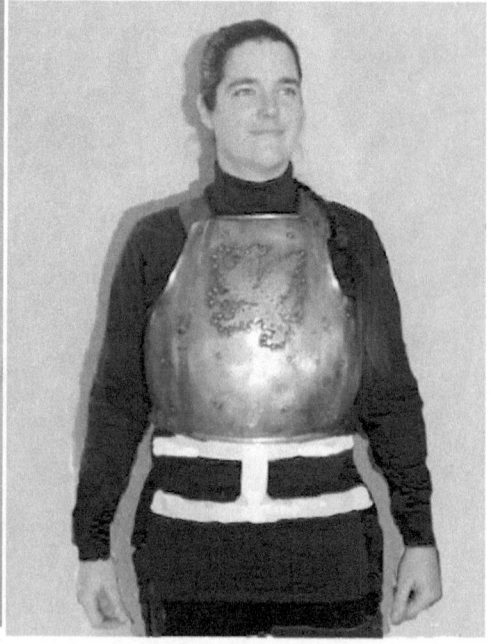

If she can touch her toes, bring her elbows together in front of her and touch her elbow to opposite knee out of armor, she should be able to do it in armor as well. The following pictures show some examples of very effective body armor. These are not the only ones out there, they are just some samples of what others have found to be effective. (Figure 3)

The distance between her hips and waist make one more important adjustment necessary. Her hips will seem more exposed than normal. The picture of the C-leg belt in Figures 3c & 3d shows a method of attaching solid legs to a hip belt. The belt wraps around the hips and distributes the weight evenly. This design prevents pulling at the small of the back and is extremely comfortable for long wear. It also provides excellent hip protection. The belt is made of two layers of thin or one layer 8-ounce leather. (It's a good design for men too. The second one is my husband's.) This pattern can include a center plate with lacing to adjust for those who fluctuate in weight. Just in case you had not noticed the similarities on your own, the pattern evolved from a garter belt. Think about it, Women have had hundreds of years to perfect a means of holding hose in place and keep them from twisting. What is leg armor but very sturdy hose? So, let's take a page from fashion and mimic what they know about legs and hose and apply it to holding up our armored legs.

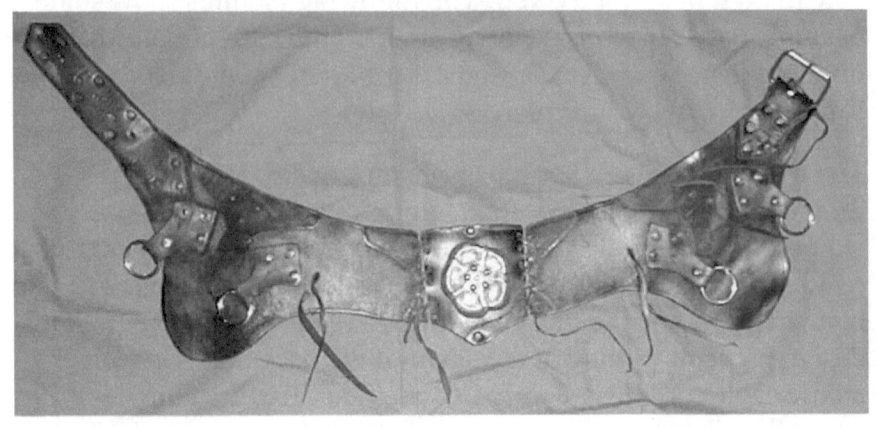

Figure 3c

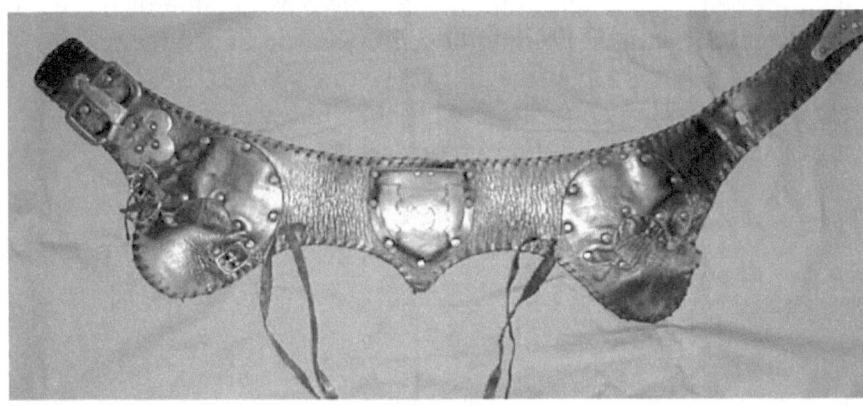

Figure 3d

The Hand

The next area to examine is the hand. Men and women each have them, but they are different. These are not the cosmetic differences of smoother skin and longer nails, these are the structural differences in how the fist is created. Make a fist as if you were going to hit someone. Now, turn your fist thumb up and look at it.

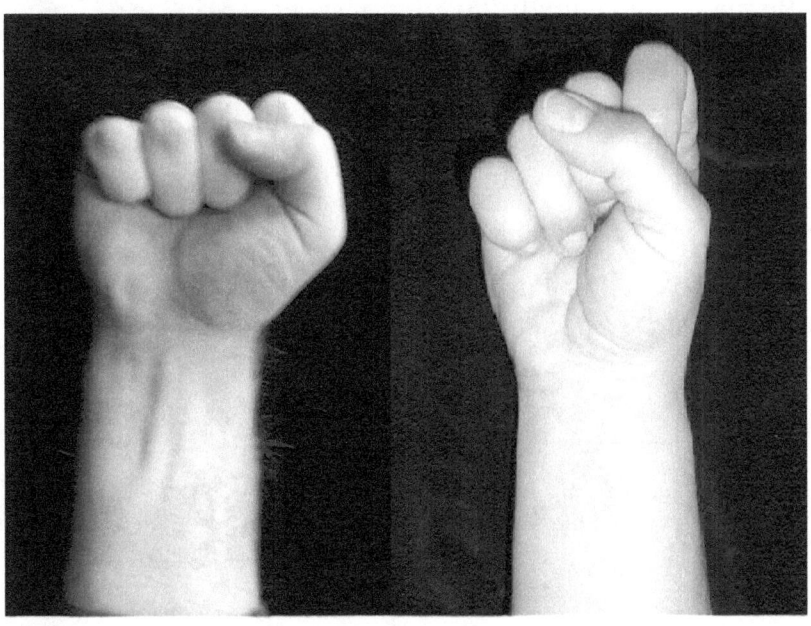

95%.[14] of the male fists look like the first picture below. (Figure 4) The knuckles make a flat line across the top of the fist, and the radial bone lines up with the second knuckle. This is _his_ strong grip. 95% of female fists look like the second picture below. (Figure 5) The first knuckle is at the highest point and the other knuckles slope down toward the pinky. The radial, the larger bone in the forearm, is lined up with the first knuckle, and the hand seems to be tilted. This is _her_ strong grip. Many women make this fist when boxing, hitting or other physical activity and her very helpful, usually male, instructor points out that if she hits something with that fist she will break her hand. It is more accurate to say that he would break his hand if he were to hit something with that fist, so, he naturally corrects it to what he knows from experience will work. (If she has been fighting for a long time do this test with the off hand. Her sword hand has probably already been "warped" into a male grip.)

Let's go through her first fighter practice:

"Hold the sword naturally" he says. She does so, in the 135 degree grip. "No, no, like this." He corrects the grip to 90 degrees, after all, his experience shows that this grip works. "Now this is how you do a flat snap, go ahead and hit the pell." She does.

"Um, this is a little uncomfortable."

"Don't worry, you will get use to it." He knows that fighting can be uncomfortable.

---

[14] All percentages of male and female physical differences derive from autopsy reports and the likelihood of identifying the gender of a body given only that body part. Personal interview with Tacoma WA, Coroner. 1993.

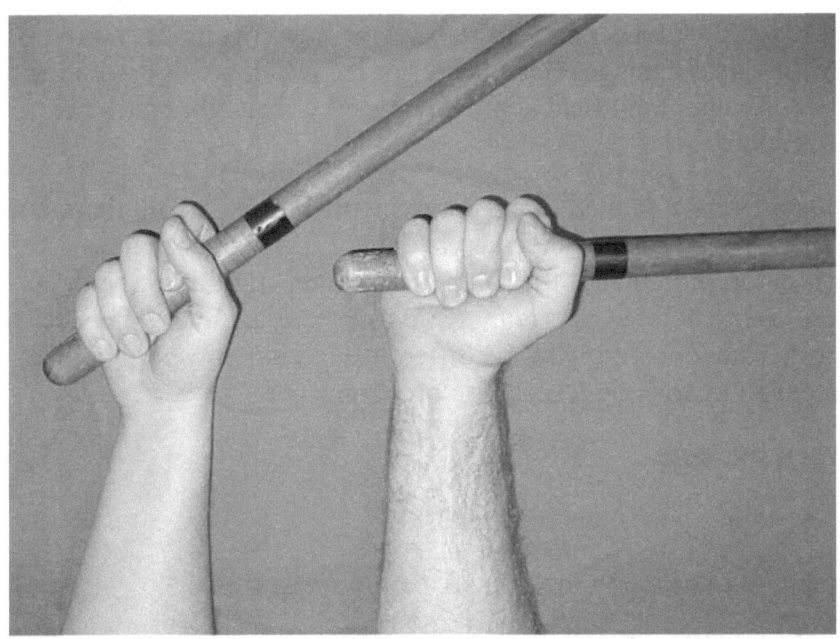

Gentlemen, here is a hint: Men and women regard pain differently. Normally the male body does not have pain unless there is some kind of injury or disease. When there is some form of pain causing damage there is a remedy to take care of it. And men do take care of it, usually as quickly as possible. Women are in a constant state of discomfort with their bodies, for the most part they ignore it, because they have lived with it and the pain is normal. Every 25 days her body contracts her internal muscles so hard that her body literally rips itself apart from the inside, and it does this for three days or so. It is not my intent to incur a penalty for roughing the reader with unnecessary information, but it is an example of the extent of the difference in pain tolerance. Researchers have known for a very long time that women have a higher threshold of pain. If men had children, "we would die out as a race in a single generation" says the old joke. If you still have doubts, try an experiment as did the military; [15] they

---

[15] ♦ (personal note – never volunteer for a military experiment.) The study involved thousands of subjects and is not based soley on my own experience (although it does match mine). Study results were still classified in 1995, and are unknown today, although additional research is readily available on this subject.

discovered that ice water inflicts the most pain without leaving any physical damage. Get a cooler of ice water and ask a man and women to put their hands in the water. See which tolerates the pain better.

This may have looked like a masochistic digression, but there is a point. She has also placed a great deal of faith in her male instructor, more about that in the chapter on emotions. She does not want to be seen as a wimp who can't play this very physical sport. That, coupled with the difference in pain threshold helps create an interesting translation problem.

When she said:

"Um, this is a little uncomfortable."

It should translate in male speak/neural system to:

"OH MY GOD! MY ARM IS BROKEN!"

If you are the male teacher and are still a little skeptical or have a morbid curiosity just how uncomfortable her "uncomfortable" is, hold the sword in her grip, and hit the pell as hard as you can. You will only do this once.

The instructor, however, just told her that this is normal and she will get use to it. She trusts him, he is trying to help her. She has dealt with other pains before and got use to them, so, she will work on getting use to this as well. She continues to hit the pell, and it continues to hurt. After a few shots she reverts to the grip that she has used for her entire life and hits the pell again. This time, the sword, because of the different angle, hits the pell before the power is delivered in the shot. It would be just like stepping into a shot to take the opponent's power out of it. This time, it felt better, but there wasn't any power in the shot. She might hear: "Well, the first couple of shots were fine, but then you lost the power." Read: You hit like a girl. "What we need to do is work on the pell some more." Ouch!

There are all sorts of styles out there that advocate using only the first couple of fingers or the last finger and thumb or a number of other variations. However, in this demonstration, at the moment of impact when the force of the shot is transmitted from the sword to the opponent, the hand is closed in a fist. Most likely it is closed in your natural fist. If it did not, the sword would bounce out of your hand. This discussion is about the moment of impact, when the fist is closed around the grip of the sword.

Many trainers maintain that they do not teach such specifics as hand closure, foot alignment and swing; they direct the student to do what is natural. In this case, nothing is natural and as a starting point he or she will imitate what the instructor is doing. Even if the instructor does not specifically teach a motion, he does teach it by example, and she will learn by imitation. To overcome this, the instructor must recognize and be able to explain the difference and how it affects fighting

The solution is to learn what the natural grip is before fighting, and work with her in developing the shots that work with her grip. This is the fighter will return to when tired or pressed. When the grip is different the sword is at a different angel, and the blow will line up differently as well. Figures 7 and 8 show what the alignment is for a flat snap in a male grip and a female grip. The sword comes to the target sooner and her hand does not need to cross her body nearly as far as his. Every shot will be slightly different and presents a challenge for the instructor to re-engineer the basic blows for her hands. The trick is to have her line up and throw blows in a form that fits HER body, not the instructor's body. The chapter "Blocks and Blows" gives a few examples of where to start with some of the basic blows. Don't worry, we a have lot more challenges for the instructor to come.

Women who have fought for some time already may now make a fist that looks like the male fist. They have been trained into this fist and it may not be their natural one. The way to find out is for her to make a fist with her off hand and see which it looks like. Since humans are basically symmetrical creatures her hand

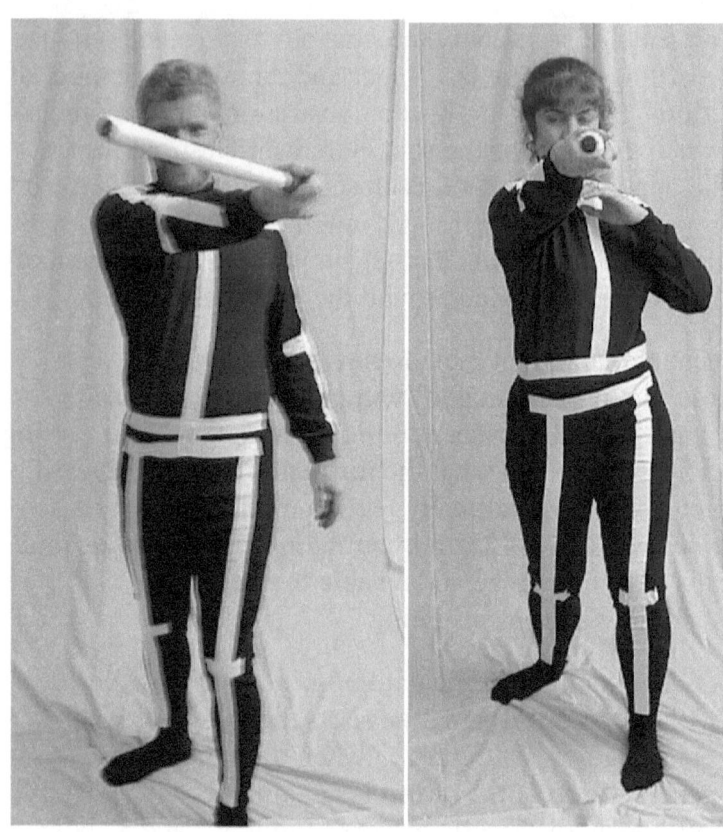

probably started out in the "female" grip, if her off hand uses that grip. If her off hand looks more like the male grip, she may be in that 5% cross over that each gender has. If her sword hand is already trained to a male grip she has a difficult and important choice to make. With the grip she has been trained to use, she will likely reach a plateau that will take longer and longer to leave. It will be difficult to maintain power in a flurry or a pressed fight. She may have to take a step before throwing a shot or be unable to make effective combinations. She must make the choice to continue with what she knows, or change and relearn taking a step back until her mind and body adjust. This is not an easy choice. I can report the success of many that have forced themselves to relearn and took off to new heights in their fighting, but it has to be a conscious effort, knowing that there will have to be a readjustment period.

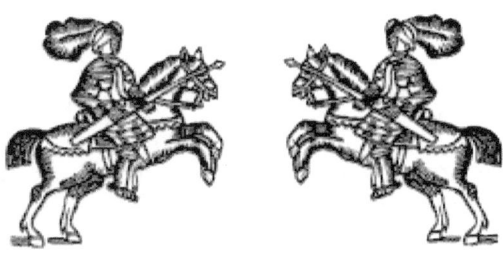

The Arm

There are a number of subtle differences in the male and female tendon structure in the arms and shoulders. Most of the differences show up in subtle movements that are more comfortable for the structure of the person doing them. For instance, ask a man to look at his nails he is likely to curl his fingers and turn his palm up. She will probably flex her fingers and look at them palm out. Asked to look at the bottom of the foot, he will likely tip his foot in front of him in a figure four and she will bend her knee and glance over her shoulder.

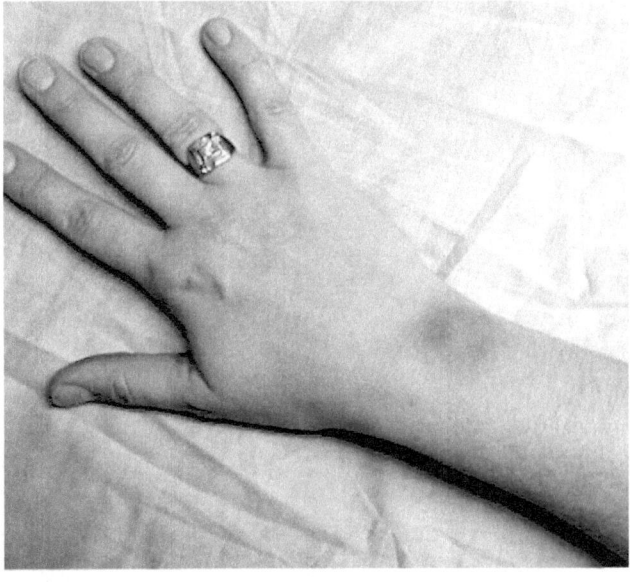

Asked to touch the collar bone he will likely touch the hand to the same shoulder, she will cross the body to touch the other shoulder. They are each doing motions that are the most comfortable for the body they are in.

These examples are very subtle; a more dramatic one can be seen when adding muscle mass to the equation. Imagine a 175-lb. woman, a 175-lb man and a 175-lb orangutan. They each have a similar muscle mass. She can curl 40-50 lbs, he might curl 75-85 lbs, and the orangutan can curl the man. The reason stems from the placement of the tendons and the way the bones set into the joints. The wider the tendons and deeper the joint lever the more power is generated from the same muscle mass.

What this translates to in fighting is a few subtle differences in

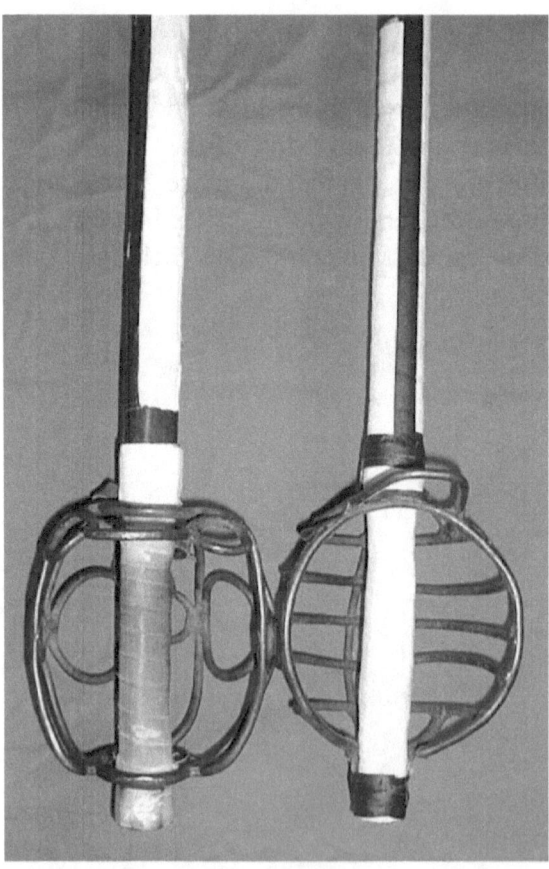

the way the wrist and arm attach and how she is likely to have a tendency to use her natural levers. Most women when they start swinging a sword with a metal basket hilt get a characteristic bruise on the back of the wrist. (Figure 9) The bruise is caused by the angle of her wrist in proportion to her arm. Look once again at the picture of her grip in figure 5 and note that not only is her fist at a slant, but it is at a different angle to the forearm, when compared to his.

His forearm and pinky are almost in a straight

line, where her forearm and pointer finger form a straight line on her fist. To accommodate the difference, the blade of her sword looks as if it is off at an angle when compared to his. Figure 10 shows a male and female sword made in the same style. The male sword has the black edge marked at the center of the opening of the basket hilt.

The female sword has the black edge marked to the far left, (this is a right handed sword). To avoid this bruise, sight down the sword from the top and rotate the basket hilt about 35 degrees, toward the body. (Figure 11a,b) I say "toward the body" as this description works with both right and left handers. In addition there is a side benefit of turning the hilt around the blade. When using the sword she will find the increased advantage that she will not hit flat as often. In the past she probably twisted her wrist to land the blade properly. When she gets tired, pressed, or excited, she may loose that last little muscle control to make the blade land sharp and as a result lands flat at the worst possible time. This adjustment not only eliminates the bruise, but, again helps prevent shots from landing flat. From the male hand perspective, it will look completely off and seem like she will hit flat every time, it will also look outrageously open in the back of the hand, but this is her body not his. Some adjustment may be needed one way or the other for her particular body . . .

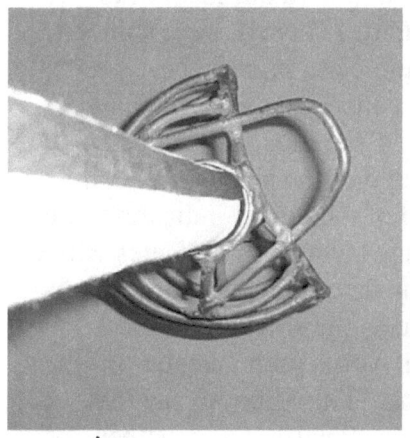 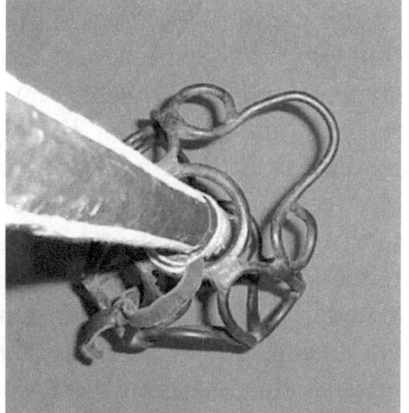

experiment.

The angel of the hand on the arm also effects the shield. The arm has a natural position it wants to rest in when holding a shield. One of the most energy efficient methods to carry a shield is to strap it in the position where the body will be most comfortable.

To do this get in the en guard stance and hold out the arm to where it is comfortable for you. (Figure 13) Next, have someone else hold up the shield where it should be to provide best coverage. Have the assistant draw around your arm, to show where the straps should go. To help place the handle strap, suspend a dowel from the leading edge of the shield and let in dangle freely. (Figure 14) The angel of the dowel indicates were to put the handle or strap. The outline of the arm indicates where the remainder of the shield strapping should go. Make sure to put some padding where the forearm meets the shield to reduce impact busing. Needless to say, this works with a heater or other strapped shields, but not with a round. This is not to say that you could not use a round. Like all things, experiment, try other shields, you may find one that is better for you than another, don't be limited by what is used in your area by 'the guys', use the one that works best for your body.

The last item to note in the difference between men and women's shoulders and arms is that different movements are stronger and more natural to her. One of the most natural is the crooked arm bent across the chest (imaging carrying a baby). This strength lends itself easily to developing a very smooth Rising Wrap Shot. This shot is demonstrated in the "Blocks and Blows" chapter as sequence 7, the Rising Wrap. The movement is very fluid and comfortable with her. Even though this is often considered an advanced shot for the average male, it may be advantageous to incorporate this early in her training due to the ease with which her body is likely to adapt to it. [16]

---

[16] Personal note: If you are the trainer, invest in those wuss flaps that cover the back of the leg.

The Hip

Most of us are aware that women's hips are wider than a man's when viewed in proportion to the shoulders. On average, she has wider hips - he has wider shoulders. It's another of those things that men often like about women. There are also a couple more differences. The pelvic girdle is also deeper front to back and tilted at an angle, when compared to a man's. Because the femur is set into the female hipbone deeper, the rotation and movement are also slightly different.

Let's go back to that first fighter practice. Figure 15 shows the basic beginner stance. Sword foot back, shield foot forward, sword back at the shoulder. There are many variations on the stance. The foot may be a little more to one side or a little more in line, the sword may be down the back or with the pommel facing the opponent, the shield may be more in line or covering the body. Slight differences aside, most new fighters are taught this as the basic stance, or something close to it. If you are left handed, hold the picture to a mirror, it should look familiar. Now he throws that flat snap. The shot comes from the shoulder area, across the body and ends with the sword striking the opponent's head. The pictures in sequence here are included to provide an idea of the motion of the shot. The final picture is the one that we will examine the closest.

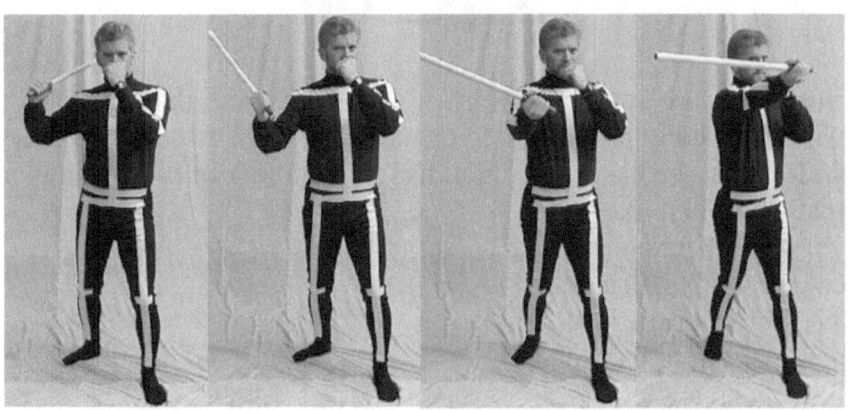

(Figure 16) Note that when the shot is finished, at the moment of impact, when the energy of the blow is to be transferred to the opponent, the hips and shoulders are aligned. If we draw a line between the shoulders and between the hips, the lines are basically parallel with each other.

When the hips and shoulders are aligned this way it provides the most stable position from which to transfer the impact to the opponent. Some excellent fighters will have the sword moving one way and the shield another, the hips rotate one direction and the shoulders are already moving in another direction setting up the next shot. But, at the moment of impact, even if the hips are moving clockwise and the shoulders counterclockwise, even the best of fighters line up the hips and shoulders for the split second it takes to transfer the power of the blow. Here at the basic level, the same building block is in place, the hips and shoulders are aligned when the blow is delivered. This is a very strong stance and effectively provides excellent positioning for power as well as defense. The effectiveness of this stance is why it is usually taught first.

Now, let's have her first lesson: Take the same stance, after all it is proven and extremely effective. She is given the same instruction on foot placement, and shown the same flat snap. Because her femur is set further into the hip socket it stops rotating when it is near flat to the opponent, but the shoulders continue with the motion in order to carry the sword forward. When the blow is finished, her hips are pointed forward and her shoulders farther to the side. The back hip is canted down and the knee twisted. The shoulders and hips are not in alignment with each other, and less power is transferred.

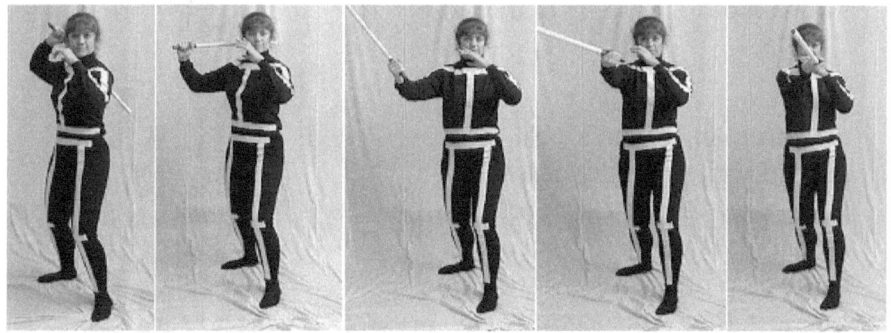

Our models are not in armor and have the points of the joints marked to make the movements more definable. Without these aids, it is not surprising to find that most trainers do not notice why the shot does not quite come out the same. What has happened is that the first part of the blow started out all right, but then her hips locked in place, as they are designed to do. In order to finish the blow she had to start working against her body and started to transfer the momentum of her shot to fight her locked hips and not into the sword. The alignment, essential to the transfer of power, is lost.

There are a few more things to notice about her finishing position. In order to get the sword to the target, the shield shoulder must come back, helping promote the shield being in the wrong place for protection. She can fight this in order to get it back in place, but in doing so, she is again fighting her own momentum and taking even more power from her shots. Her trainer is likely to try to correct the problem by telling her to put more hip into it, she does and begins to feel pain in the lower back as her hips jar even harder into the locked position. The last item to note is that her leg is twisted with the foot on the ground and a significant amount of torque is applied to the sword side knee. This is a very uncomfortable position and frankly, is not all that effective. Again, when she says that the drill is uncomfortable, she is assured that this is normal and that in time she will get use to it. The answer is somewhat unconventional, particularly when viewed from a male body perspective. Place the sword foot forward. (Figure 19)

Stop thinking about all the places that this opens up the defense in a male body for the moment, and let's look at the new stance step by step. With the sword foot forward, throw the same flat snap. (Figure 20)

Note that this time her hips and her shoulders are lined up with each other in the desired position to transfer power. She has not spent half the power of her shot fighting her own body. The shield is pulled in front of the body, protecting it. She can now

"put her hips into the shot" without being jarred to a stop. Many of the phrases that are commonly used to describe the "flow" of a shot such as "Uncoil like a spring", "Allow the sword to be an extension of the arm" and "Throw the energy out the tip of the sword" will start to make more sense as she experiences the smooth transfer of power that is not there when using the traditional male stance.

As with all new things the openings and defenses will be different. The shield may need to come more forward to compensate for the sword foot, the fighter may have to be more mobile. Each person will be different in how they best use the basic building blocks. The sum total lesson here is that the sword foot forward offers her better position, defense, and power base than the sword foot back. This is due to her tendon and bone structure in her hip and shoulder. If you are a male instructor, do not expect this modification to look or feel comfortable on your body, you just are not built the same.

An interesting thing to note is that she is also likely to have a butt.......stop laughing. Now think of the body as a counter balance, she has to have something to balance out the weight there, and make it so she can stand with her weight evenly distributed on her feet. To do this, she is likely to have her shoulders more forward, and well, her arm is attached to her shoulder, and her shield is attached to her arm. The end result is that the shield is more forward than it is on a comparable male, and that leg is not nearly as open as it looks.

There is a note of caution here, when she changes her stance, re-calibrate. Up until now, she has been able (if she is a fighter already) to tell how good the blow is by how much it hurt to throw. This may be a foreign concept for most men, but it is true for most women. Oddly, some women fight me on this point, because they have nothing to compare it to, until it does not hurt – and all of the energy goes into the opponent and not their own body. The blow may feel to light to her, but she will no longer be fighting her own body and far more power will be transferred to the blow. Several women have reported denting armor with what they thought had been nothing more than an average shot.

Another advantage of the shifted stance is the extended reach.

Many good fighters know that when the sword foot is forward there are several inches more in the reach of the blow. Try this experiment: Take a sword foot back stance and throw a shot. Mark where the tip of the sword reaches.

(Figure 21a)

Now, shift stance, without moving the body, and throw the same blow. (Figure 21b) You will note that the sword is several inches farther out than before. Since most women are generally shorter than most men, this is also a distinct advantage. Good fighters tend to judge whether they are in range based on the distance to the person's shoulders, and they forget to look at the feet. When the sword foot is forward, the fighter has several extra inches reach and the fighter who thought they were out of range is not.

(Figure 21b)

This is not always the best stance for a women to learn first, but it often is, simply because it is easier for her to develop good power generation with it. One of the problems comes in that this is usually considered a more advanced style for a man. And most male instructors teach what works for them. Give it a try. Have her haul off and hit the shield with the shield foot forward two or three times, then try it with the sword foot forward. Allow the person being hit to determine which blows were stronger. Often it is sword foot forward. If there is no obvious feel in difference, look at which way has her hips and shoulders in line with each other at the moment of impact. This will tell you what will be the stronger stance for her in the beginning.

I've said it a few times already, and hinted at it a few more, but let me come out and say it again - - this is not the only style she can fight in. In fact, eventually she should learn shield foot forward, or no foot forward, just like every other advanced fighter……she should be able to work with whatever the situation and ground gives her. But in the beginning, try the one that is easiest to develop good form and power, it will provide a huge leg up in the long run.

For many years we have attempted to teach male and female students the same, not realizing that the body mechanics are very different. Many a trainer has worked and worked only to find that the female students are extremely slow to develop. It's as if they have a tendency to stay in the category of "new fighter" a very long time, in spite of the work that they put into practice. If a male student were to start fighting and receive training in the hardest stance and style first, he too would remain pell meat for a very long time. If he then looked around at others who started at the same time, but developed faster, he might think he was the one with the problem. The sword foot back is one of the hardest styles for her, the sword foot forward far more basic and strong. Work with your female student to develop the stance and style that fits her structure, it is difficult, but she is up for the challenge if you are.

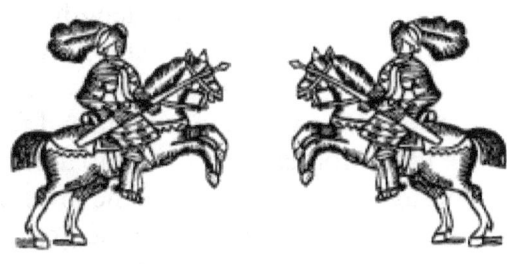

The Hipbone is connected to the Leg Bone

After extensive discussion on the hips and the differences, it only seems natural to look at the differences associated with the leg. It is no illusion that women proportionally have longer legs than men. Look at the pictures in figure 22 and notice that he makes up more of his height in the body, she in the leg. Also notice that the angle from her hip bone to her knee is less perpendicular than his is and more angled to accommodate the wider hip and deeper set hip socket.

This increased angle has a tendency to apply more pressure to the knee joint than might normally be expected. As a result, care should be taken when learning movement and stance and generating power. Any discomfort in the knee needs to be addressed with a change in stance immediately. It is interesting to note that more women than men suffer from ACL (Anterior Crucieve Ligament) damage in the knee due to the additional stress, but only 10% of the corrective surgeries are on women.[17]

---

[17] Personal interview with Dr. Steve Crenshaw, Orthopedic Surgeon, Madagain Army Hospital, Ft. Lewis Washington, 1994.

The other difference to address here is the length of the femur, or thighbone. Because the bone is proportionally larger, using a man's leg pattern for armor and adjusting for her size does not make the best fit. The pattern needs to be adjusted for the thigh. One last note here; most women won't want to admit it, but they have a small fat roll just above and behind the knee. If the standard pattern is used, when she drops to the ground, the armor will pinch and bruise this spot. (Figure 23) Any good armorer can make the adjustments, if he knows to tweek these spots.

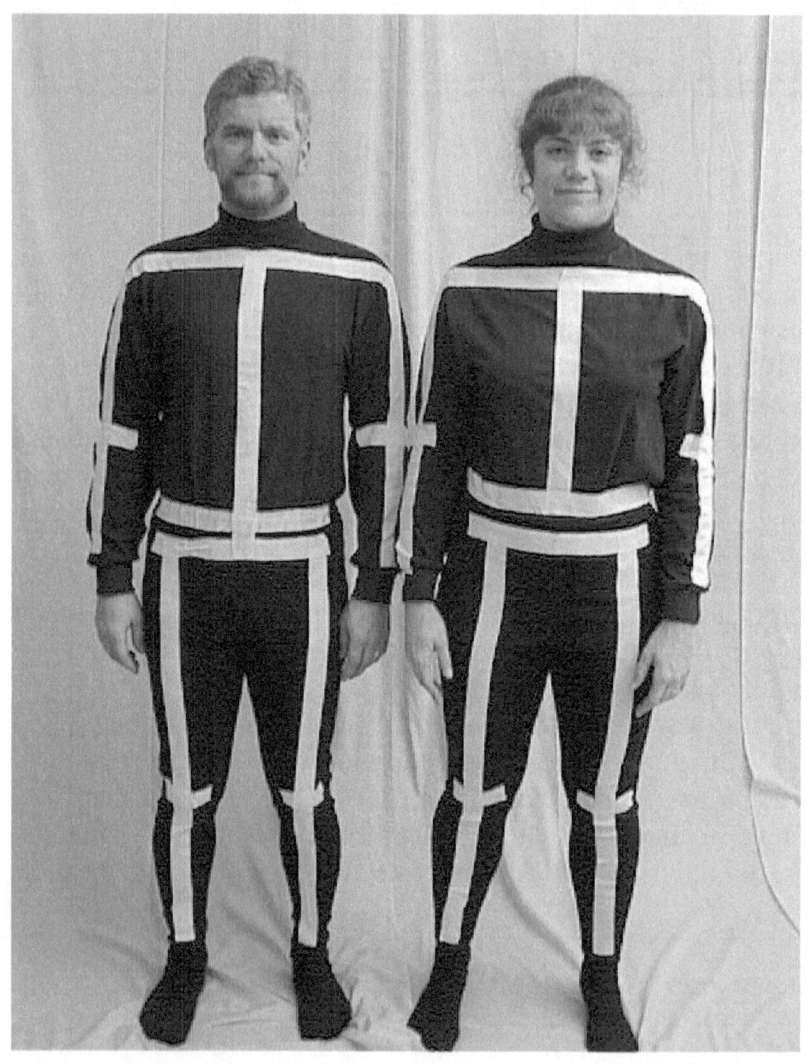

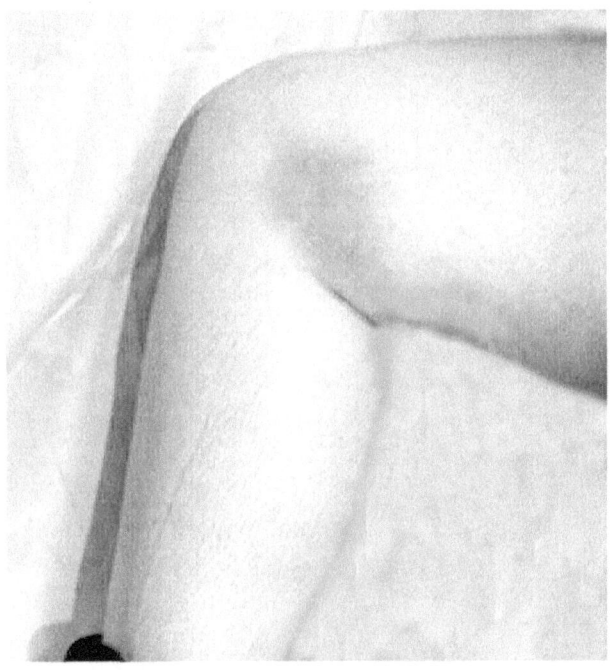

An armoring friend was making a full rig for a female friend. He took measurements and began his work. He said that while constructing the body and legs he stopped every few minutes convinced that he was doing something wrong. He resisted the impulse to add this here or take this off there and forced himself to make the suit according to her measurements. When it was ready for delivery he was convinced that it was an atrocity, but it fit her perfectly. He still has a hard time believing that the measurements could be so drastically different.

Hand-me-down armor is great, but it generally does not do well for women. Her body is enough different that the armor will need to be hand-me-downs from other women, who have had the armor fitted in the first place. Take the time to get the right armor, in the end she will enjoy fighting much more in a rig that does not hurt when she moves. The appendix shows a variety of armor types and a few patterns that work well.

II. Physiological

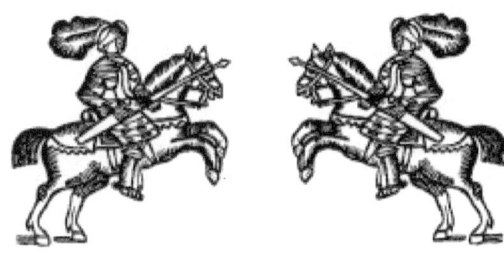

Understanding Chemistry

In addition to a host of physical differences large enough to see, there are ones far too small to see, but that have at least as great an effect on how the different sexes approach fighting. These are the chemical differences between men and women. To illustrate how significant chemical differences are, let's look at the drastic changes that testosterone and estrogen have in the body.

Most of us recognize testosterone as the chemical that makes the two celled organism we start out being turn into men and estrogen the one that develops us into women. This chemical difference is responsible for making the physical sexual characteristic differences. The lack of estrogen in the body creates the physical and emotional upheaval that often accompanies menopause. Anyone who does not think that the chemicals in the body have an effect on emotional balance has never seen a woman go through the "change of life", or a boy adolescence.

Within the last thirty years, researchers have found evidence to suggest hormones also effect the production of other chemicals. Just how much effect and on what other chemicals is a topic of current research and debate in the medical community, and is likely to be for another thirty years to come. One of the agreed upon effects is that testosterone based life forms, men, have smaller amounts of Serotonin[18] than their estrogen based counterparts Serotonin helps regulate the secretions of the adrenal glands.

****

Warning: Boring semi-technical description of chemicals and how they work in your body to follow, you may wish to skip this part.

****

The Adrenal glands are triangular-shaped glands located at the top surface of each kidney, which secretes through the blood flow in the kidneys. These glands produce three chemicals, or more properly catecholamines; Dopamine, Norepinephrine, and Epinephrine. Dopamine is released in the body and helps shut down various systems enabling a person to sleep.[19] For the other two, allow me to quote from Taber's Cyclopedic Medical Dictionary:

> The adrenal medulla is under the control of the sympathetic nervous system and functions in conjunction with it. It is intimately related to adjustments of the body in response to emotional states. Anticipatory states tend to bring about the release of norepinephrine. More intense emotional reactions, especially those in response to extreme stress, tend to increase the secretion of both norepinephrine and epinephrine; epinephrine is

---

[18] **serotonin** – A chemical, 5-hydroxytryptamine (5-HT), present in platellets, and mast cells. Involved in neural mechanisms. Taber's Medical Dictionary, F.A. Davis Company, Philadelphia, Edition 14.

[19] Just as a side note, turkey has been found to help stimulate and release Dopamine in the system. The lesson here is if you have a boring meeting or lecture after lunch, don't have that turkey sandwich.

important in mobilizing the physiological changes that occur in the "fight or flight" response to emergency situations.

According to the same dictionary epinephrine is another way of saying adrenaline.

Seretonin is a powerful vasoconstrictor and can prevent the production and dispersal of adrenaline leading to physical reaction, in this case the flight or fight response. In short, the more Estrogen in the body, the more Seretonin. The more Seretonin in the system, the slower the body secretes and processes adrenaline. This effect seems to be true from birth. A recent study at Children's Hospital in Boston found boy babies are more emotionally expressive and girls more reflective. Boys have "lower levels of the neurotransmitter Serotonin, which inhibits aggression and impulsivity." This study also suggests that girls are more innately able to control their emotions.[20]

****

End Technical Warning Here

****

So, what all this means is that if you have more testosterone in your system, you are less likely to be in chemical control of your emotional "on" button. The graphs below help to illustrate the effects on adrenaline in men and women. I know that you never thought you would have to do this again after you left High

---

[20] Newsweek: Building a better Boy, May 1998 quoting study by Boston's Children's Hospital, 1997.

School, but bare with it a moment, it really is useful in explaining the point.

Men, have a tendency to release and process adrenaline in the system fairly quickly. Point "0" is the stimulus; she left the towel on the floor, cap off the toothpaste, maybe used his razor blade. Whatever the circumstance, he is upset. Man hits his adrenaline high within 30 seconds and "blows up". Maybe he storms off, but in less than ten minutes he is back to something close to normal and can discuss the problem.

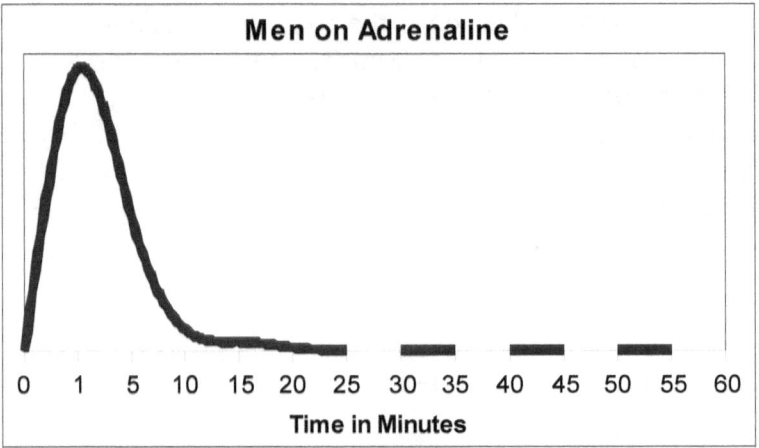

She, however is a different creature, with a different chemical composition. She looks something like this:

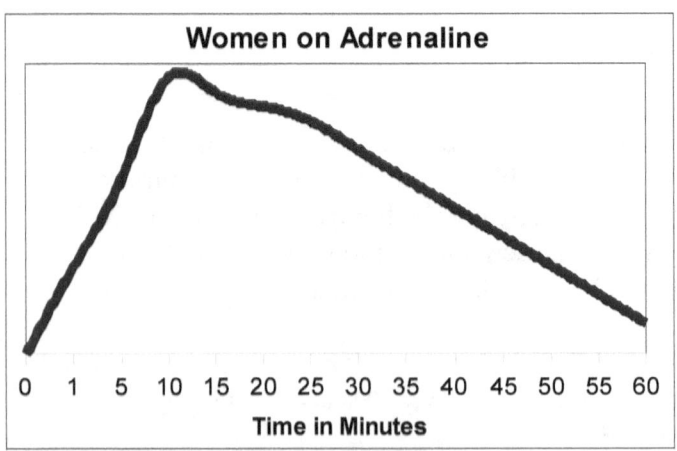

Her reaction to the same stimulus is more likely to follow the above chart. The Serotonin in her system inhibits the fast emotional outburst that her male counterpart had. Instead, she sets out for a slow steam. Unfortunately, the same things that prevented the adrenaline from being released in her system in the first place also prevent it from being cleaned out and "burned off". So, while slow to boil, once there, she has a tendency to stay steamed for nearly an hour or more.

Just in case you have not already put the two together[21], let's see what the charts look like when compared with each other.

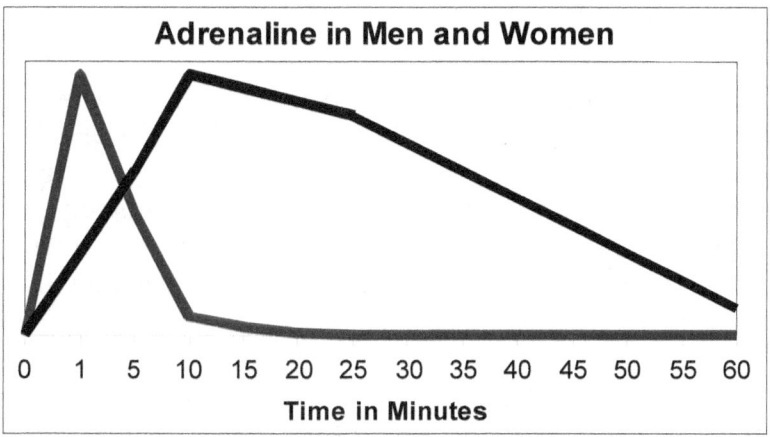

At this point, you may see a trend. He and she have a fight over the toilet seat, drinking out of the carton, which way the toilet paper roll goes, or whatever happens to spring up in the discussion, and he reacts with intense anger and shuts down, walks out, or maybe just fumes for a bit. In ten minutes or so, he's ready to come back and discuss the issue rationally, just about the time she is reaching her emotional high of being angry.

---

[21] On an interesting note, this chart is also representative of the two paths that men and women take in sexual arousal and orgasm. For the same reasons. Masters and Johnson study as quoted in <u>Human Sexual Behavior</u>, Dr. Clare Hammer, 1991.

Often, he is confused and can't understand why she is still upset over whatever it was that set off the argument in the first place.

With this in mind, recognize that biologically, he and she will approach a tournament differently. He can often use his adrenaline and natural heightening of senses which gives him as a tool when he fights. If she is taught to do the same thing, she is not likely to derive any benefit from it until several minutes after she is off the field. She has two options. She can warm up about ten minutes before her first fight and be on that adrenaline "high" by the time she is on the field. Or, she can learn to fight in a serious stone cold manner. The later has some interesting psychological advantages.

Most men, when coming to the field, are playing a game when they fight. To see an opponent who is not playing, but instead is taking this very real, is a little unnerving. Men rarely see women fight, and having a serious female opponent can be extremely intimidating, in part because they remember the last catfight they saw. They don't want to be on the receiving end of that kind of altercation.

Any bartender or bouncer will tell you that men and women fight differently. Men have stages they go through. They posture, and puff up and make a few idle insults and eventually get around to stepping outside to "take care of business". At any point along the way in this ritual they can back down and have a drink, often with each other. Women are different. Unlike the man who came to shouting quickly and postures while he decides what to do, she already knows. In fact, she has been steaming there for about ten minutes or so and is finally ready for action. Her fight is more like "Bitch!" "Slut!" BANG! call this "0 to Uzi in 2.3 seconds". If she does fight, the fighting looks completely different, they go for the eyes, yank hair and are generally all out nasty. Is it any wonder why he might remember that and not want to be on the receiving end? Her fights are too serious, they are not the game he is expecting.

Chemical changes have a very real and profound effect on physical action. Every woman first learns how to work with her own body and its chemical changes during her monthly cycle. For some the answer is to eat certain foods, others need to stay away from some foods. Some women want extra sleep, some less, still others crave exercise. However she deals with the chemical changes in her body from month to month, she learned to do so through experimentation, trial and error. The same holds true in this case. There is no one right answer for all women. Experiment. Recognize that this too is an area to explore and develop in fighting. Do you warm up ahead of time and have the adrenaline in the system when you fight? Do you fight better without it? Do you fight every ten minutes to refresh the adrenaline? These are questions you will have to find out about yourself. As a trainer, make note of when she fights better and what happened *before* she fought. An informed outside opinion can be invaluable.

III. Psychological

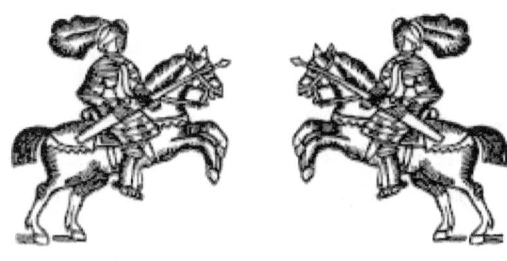

The Lizard Brain

Now that we have explored some of the physical and physiological differences, let's look a little closer at emotional and psychological differences.

At first I considered this to be a daunting task. I had always been taught that everyone was unique, that we each faced the world with a different outlook. It's one of the great strengths of a community, many viewpoints have the opportunity to provide many different solutions to the same problem. Then I started taking some "think outside the box" training, and I started to wonder "What created the box?". The answer is simpler than expected. We were each conditioned by the same society. Someone who grew up three thousand miles from where I did on the opposite side of the country still watched the same TV programs I did, they experienced the same world events, economic depression, latest inventions and fads. These items shape the society we live in and this in turn shapes the next generation.

We have each been conditioned by our society, and by and large, that society has left some programming on how men and women should behave with each other. Women in general are taught not to compete, not to excel and not to look to good when compared to men. At this point it is easy to say "I was taught differently, I was taught that I could do anything a man could." Frankly, I was too. If you were fortunate enough to have this king of upbringing, great, it just makes you more confused. Confusion can ultimately lead to understanding, so this in and of itself is not necessarily a bad thing. In this case the confusion comes from what the rest of the world taught us.

Even if the parents raise independent women, the society we live in does not. We have each been conditioned with the society-accepted behavior. Our parents were part of the conditioning, but only a small part, some believe as little as 5%. The other 95% of our conditioning came from school, church, friends, friend's parents, TV, books and so on. If you have any doubt left at all, ask the mother of any child who just started school. It's amazing what new things that child learns from society today and how it is interpreted in the mind of the child. What did those things teach us?

Within each of us there is something I refer to as the Lizard Brain. It is that piece of us that develops our morals, standards and emotional responses. It is part Ego, part "Hind Brain", and part "Inner Child". It is the part that shapes our personality. There is an old saying, "Show me the boy and I will show you the man." It refers to what researchers have found in child development. The basic personality of a human is created before they turn seven. These morals, values and motivations are what I call the Lizard Brain.

The Lizard Brain is filled with the learning that we picked up from observation at the school yard, watching our parents, other adults in the store or street, watching TV, and even some in the class room. I remember my parents being very progressive about what I learned and the messages I received about what I could grow up to be. But I also remember the books my elementary teacher read to us in first grade. You may find it or one similar to it in schools today it reads:

    What will I be when I grow up?

Boys can be Doctors, Girls can be Nurses.

Boys build houses, Girls keep houses clean.

Boys fix things, Girls need things fixed.

You get the picture. This book and others like it are still very much in circulation in the schools today. Even books with publishing dates in the 90s have very much the same message, though not as obvious. This is not a treatise on the appalling state of our educational system, that is another book in itself, but this should be an adult's window on what you learned as a child, before you were even aware of learning.

Many of us have heard of the poem "All I ever needed to know, I learned in kindergarten". In some respect this is true, a part of us stopped learning shortly after this time. This is not really a bad thing, just an observation. If there was no structure in our learning process we might do something like develop morals after we understood politics. Talk about a confused person!

Update for second edition: There was a comedy show called "That '70's Show". The Episode "Battle of the Sexist" aired 9/20/98 [22] and highlighted what happens when a girl consistently beats a boy at basket ball and other games. Donna (the strong female teen) is counseled that she will never get Eric (our Male Lead) to like her if she doesn't let him win. It is presented as a comedy, and highlights the absurdity of the situation, but it does not change the facts. This was how many women today were raised. Even when the message was not as overt as it was in the 70's, the message still came through loud and clear to the Lizard Brain.

The next several chapters will take a closer look at what we have learned in those formative years from our society on how men and women should behave with each other. When it comes to fighting, there are five hurdles for the female fighter to overcome

---

[22] www.that70sshow.com, Episode Gallery First Season, fourth Episode.

before she walks on the field, as an equal to the novice male fighter. While these hurdles tend to effect women significantly, many men are completely unaware that they exist. It's not his fault that he does not face these hurdles or even understand them, after all, his programming is different. Most women, however, will identify with each of the five hurdles here and may take years to overcome them. It is my hope that they will realize that the emotional responses are normal and why they happen. The hurdles may not appear in the order described here, and they may appear too lesser or greater degrees.

To help this along, we are going to use two personifications: The first is Rose, a lady who wants to fight. The second is Lizard Brain, the part of her that was trained not to.

For the men, if you have doubt about what you are reading, grab the nearest female and ask her. For the gents I hope that you will come away with a sense of why she behaves the way she does when it comes to fighting and how to help her when she chooses to fight.

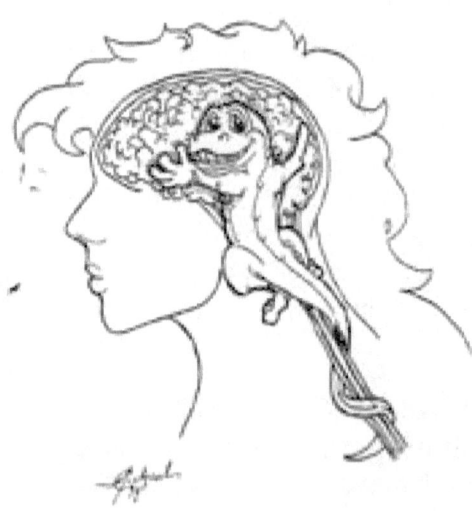

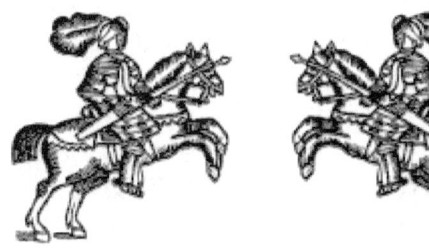

Hurdle One: I can play this game

At first blush the thought here is, well of course you can play this game, almost anyone can play. Even though we try to believe this, the thought goes directly against our programming. From a very early age, young women are taught not compete with men. Look at some of the programming with an adult perspective. Go watch Saturday morning cartoons some time, they really are fun, but instead of going to get a snack during the break, watch the commercials. Some of those commercials are the same from when I was a kid. When a group of children play a game such as Hungry Hungry Hippo©, Trouble© or Sorry©, you will see two boys and two girls playing. One of them will jump up at the end and say "I Win!". It's always a boy. No kidding. There are two notable exceptions, one is Candyland, the other Connect Four. In one, the girl is playing with an obviously younger brother, maybe half her age and mom and dad. In the other, she declares her victory and her clearly younger brother says "Pretty sneaky, Sis." So, what is the message here? She can win, but only when we keep it in the family[23] and only when she clearly overpowers the person or uses subterfuge. Neither of these tactics do we consider to be proper behavior on the tourney field.

---

[23] Look for this concept to show up again in Hurdle Number Five.

There are lots of other places we take up this instruction. Watch the cartoons, boys will race or compete with each other, but not the girls. If she does compete and win, his feelings will be hurt and she will make amends. To be fair here, we are not only teaching her Lizard Brain not to compete, but we are teaching him to feel bad, angry, upset if she does. Above all else, women are taught not to cause conflict and to amend what is wrong wherever possible. Competing causes conflict.

Now, she has decided to fight. GREAT! But, have you every noticed that it takes considerably longer for her to "Get her armor together"? From the time that she declares that she wants to fight to the time she walks on the field in armor for the first time is on the average seven times longer than it is for her male counterpart.[24] In many individual cases it takes much longer, but the average is at least seven times longer. Even if she has all the help in the world building, making or getting the armor together, she will find any number of excuses to keep from going out on the field. It has nothing to do with desire, it has to do with the war going on in her head.

Looking from the outside, the male reader may not see the depth of programming. Our society is replete with messages that she can not compete with others. Women were not allowed to compete in the Olympics until the forties, and they still don't compete against men. Over 50% of high schools across the nation do not offer sports to female students. Less than 1% of schools allow women to participate in contact sports. Aside from Jell-O wrestling, there may not be a contact sport that has more female participants than male. All professional sports divide competitions by gender, implicitly stating that the playing field can not be even between them.

---

[24] In a survey of the SCA completed by the author in 1995.

In an effort to overcome this social conditioning, Nike™ produced an award winning commercial titled "If you let me play sports". The commercial opens with a five or six year old girl looking precious, as if she were asking daddy for a favor and her voice saying "If you let me play sports. . . " Fade to the grown women in work out gear, sweaty and a little out of breath and the women's voice "I'll be 53% less likely to have breast cancer." Then another little girl "If you let me play sports . . . ." ". . . I'll be 72% more likely to leave an abusive relationship." "If you let me play sports . . ." "I'll be 85% less likely to be the victim of a violent crime." And so on. The commercials stark black and white images and contrasting message presented a powerful case for allowing sports for young girls. The little girl was begging to play, the older woman supplied the logic. Unfortunately, it was deemed too disturbing and only aired a few times.

She has been conditioned not to fight, not to compete, not to win particularly when dealing with men. And this is a man's sport. Just look out on the field, in the tournaments, mostly men? All the encouraging words in the world will not win this battle for her. They help - don't get me wrong. But those encouraging words happen at best every few days. She has lived with the Lizard Brain all her life, it's there when she eats, drives, before falling asleep, and all the quiet times. As much as she wants to believe those encouraging words, there is lots of competition for them to be heard. The Lizard Brain constantly says; *"You can't play this game." "This is a man's game, girls aren't suppose to play this sport." "Girls don't play this game for long, because they can't really do it."* She has to overcome this hurdle herself. When she has convinced herself that the Lizard Brain might be wrong, she will trust someone enough to walk onto the field to train with them.

She did not choose this trainer lightly. She is placing in this person the faith and trust to help her overcome the social conditioning that she has had bludgeoned into her. If you are this trainer, recognize this and be prepared to accept the responsibility. She is at this stage, in regards to her fighting, as vulnerable as a child. In fact, the two of you will be reprogramming part of her that still is a child. A cross word or brutal act will have long lasting and potentially damaging results, in regards to fighting. This does not mean that you should shy from the challenge. Far from it, she will likely be one of the most attentive and eager students, and this is an incredibly rewarding experience for the teacher. What this does mean is that the teacher must attempt to understand how she learns and how lessons are best taught. Men and women learn differently and the technique that is effective for him is not likely to be for her. We will go over learning styles in a little more detail as we explore the other motivational factors in the upcoming chapters.

Here she is! She has walked on the field to fight, she is ready to try to show the Lizard Brain that it could be wrong. For many men, this is no challenge at all, in fact they could not wait to get on the field. For her it has taken awhile to overcome the conditioning and now she is ready. The trainer must acknowledge this as the victory that it is, she has won the battle between the ears. Failure to see this as a triumph that it is will come back to haunt her in hurdle number four.

If she is reluctant to come to this stage and still has every excuse in the world to prevent her from practicing such as, I'm coming down with a cold, I'm working on another project, I've got some sewing to do, I need to floss the cat, or whatever she is still fighting the Lizard Brain. The excuses will be quite believable and often very good, this should be seen as an excellent display of her creativity. One or two may even be fairly accurate, but when they become a trend, the excuses are only a symptom of the greater battle. Encourage her, but don't be hurt if your words seem to fall on deaf ears at first, she did hear you, she is just weighing it against what is being said inside. Encourage her more, if possible take her to see other female fighters. For the most part, she has to fight this battle by herself. She will, give her time and encouragement.

Often, the first place she will overcome this hurdle is in private. She will often likely be able to deal with a private fighter practice with her trusted trainer, alone, sooner than she would in a group practice. This in part comes from the conditioning that she received when younger that intoned that if she was going to win, it should be kept in the family. This is a good first step, but should not be used as a crutch and should not be the only practice. If she can fight in private, move her quickly on to a full practice, even if she is only fighting the same people for now. The practice in the open is an acknowledgement that what she is doing is not shameful, part of her Lizard Brain has convinced her that it is.. If you are the trainer, let her know when you are proud of her. For him, such an acknowledgement can be seen as patronizing, to her it is validation.

Sometimes the excuse to stay in the private practice will be because she "wants to be good enough not to make a fool of herself". Be impressed with her creativity and explain that all new fighters look like new fighters. She cannot make a fool of herself. When this excuse crops up, or one that sounds much like it, it comes from the near completion of this hurdle, but not entirely. She is still trying to convince herself that it is alright to do this.

Here is a funny thing when communicating with most women. Even if all the excuses are removed, if the problem that created the excuse is not addressed, it still won't happen. In this case, all the excuses (I need to get my armor together, I want to lose 5 lbs, I have another project, the dog got out, and so on.) are a way of diverting attention from the actual problem. She does not want you to solve the excuses, just listen to them. She will eventually get around to addressing the problem herself, if you are still listening, you can help out.

Hurdle Two: I can Hit

Well, of course you can, you might say. This **is** after all a full contact sport. You can even look at the female student and see that she hits. It's a little more than that though. The symptoms of this hurdle show up as a desire to continue practice on the pell rather than fighting a person. Or when fighting a person, hitting square in the center of the opponent's shield, pulling a shot, or not taking the obvious opening. Perhaps one of the most obvious spots is when she does land a blow, immediately saying "I'm Sorry!".

Each of these symptoms is an indication that she has not yet convinced herself that it is acceptable to hit the other person. Again, much of this comes from the social conditioning that we grew up with. Go back to those commercials you grew up on. Did you ever see a girl play Rock'em Sock'em Robots© in the commercials? No, she was always shown playing with Little Baby Wet Me, or some such other nurturing toy. Her toys involved dressing, combing, grooming or nurturing another object in some way. She is conditioned in these ways to please and nurture another. Again, this in and of itself in not a bad thing, in fact it is great when considering the future necessities of taking care of the next generation. But, when it comes to fighting, this is an area that requires some reconditioning.

This may not be as easy as reprogramming the social conditioning that we each grew up with, the problem may be deeper. To be sure, conditioning is a part of the issue, but there are those who believe that the "racial memory" is linked closely to the way we fight. Consider that for as long as history has been around and before, man has gone away from the home to fight. This can be seen in the cave paintings of the La Scaugh and evidence from early historic and prehistoric archeology. Men gather as groups and go after an objective. The objective may be food, a neighboring tribe, a war, a cause or a religion. Rather traditionally these fights happen away from home. There are lots of options open to the gathering of men with an objective. They can fight, retreat, regroup, make a new plan, decide that they are not that hungry or that the Pope's need for Jerusalem is not all that great after all. The point is, they have options to fighting.

Women, on the other hand, approach the problem differently. As the Gatherer half of the Hunter/Gather species that we are, the female has tended to stay with the less mobile younger members of the tribe, or just at home in the town, shire, castle, city while the able bodied men go off to fight. Just as he has options when he fights, she does not. When the intruder or threat comes to her, she is the last able body between the enemy and the next generation. She has only one of two choices, fight or let the next generation die. Since we are creatures of survival, the second option is not real good. This difference can be seen in a number of ways, even today. Remember the discussion on saratonin and how it prevented her from immediately responding with the "fight or flight" adrenaline? The adrenaline is released in her system much more slowly, and as a result she does not have the same reaction. She stays until the last possible moment.

You've seen this in a Cat Fight. Ask any bar bouncer, they will tell you that men and women fight differently. Men go through a series of posturing phases, puffing up the chest, asking if he's talking to him (of course he is), a few insults exchanged, an invitation to fight and so on. At almost any step along the way they can back down and go have a beer with each other and talk about how they would have whooped each other. Women are a little more reserved in the beginning as the adrenal glands slowly start to release the chemicals and by the time the confrontation does occur it goes from 0 to Uzi in 2.3 seconds and they are ready to kill each other. There is no opportunity to intercede, it happens too fast, from the outside perspective. From the inside perspective, she has been seething over the issue for the last ten minutes. Her fighting style is also more vicious and permanent. Remember, fighting for him is a means of socializing, bonding, building relationships, for her it is survival. She goes for the eyes, hair, and vitals, and she does not stop once her opponent is down. He usually does, after all, he has established his place in the pack, killed the food, or met the objective. She is not going to let the enemy get up, or come back at her again when she is vulnerable later.

The National Association of Police Officers concluded a study in 1991, which cataloged handgun discharges in relationship to intruders. It seems that men on the average fire two shots at the perimeter of the property when confronted with an intruder. Women tend to allow the intruder past the perimeter of the property, through the door, and into the house. If they have children, they will station themselves at the last possible exit before the children's rooms, usually at the head of the hall. Or if they are single or without children they will retreat to the bedroom or kitchen, both considered areas of "inner sanctuary" and then they will empty the clip. In fact quite a few reload and empty the weapon twice, just for good measure. You have to wonder if the intruder took ten minutes.

When it comes to fighting this hurdle is seen as someone who plays a largely defensive game. Someone who will not throw the first blow in a fight. The back of her head may be trying to convince herself that she is not yet really in the fight. She may have taken the field, saluted everyone, but she is still not in the fight. After all, everyone could get struck by lightning, they are wearing metal suits. It could happen.

When he hits her, the rules change, she is now defending herself. But she has given up a strategic advantage, the ownership of the fight. The rules change after she is hit because we are conditioned to place the man who hits a woman in the role of bad guy. This is one of those Lizard Brain problems he will have to work out. Think of it, every movie, cartoon, instance where he hits her, he is the bad guy. About the only place it is seen is when she slaps him and he slaps her back, even then he's walking the line of acceptable masculine behavior. Both sexes are conditioned that the man is not to hit the woman. For her it is one of the things that creates this stumbling block as well as the next one.

For the Trainer:

And the solution to the fear of hitting another is - practice. If she won't hit you any where but in the center of the shield, drop the shield. When she apologizes, and she will, ask why, after all, she is doing the right thing. Why apologize? When she has to recognize and acknowledge that there is no reason to be sorry, she will start to stop. Don't expect it to happen all at once, or quickly. In fact, once you point it out, she will believe that it displeases you (her trusted trainer), and she will beat herself up until she no longer does it every time you fight. She truly wants to please her trainer, mention it once or twice and move on. Constantly correcting her over something that she can not help but do will make her feel that she has failed you.

As she starts to fight more, she will realize that her armor protects her, and you as well. It eventually becomes clear that she is not really hurting her opponent. Further, they expect to get hit. This will slowly start to creep into the Lizard Brain that it is ok to hit, some people, some times, under some conditions. It's an argument that must be won in her head. All you need to do is plant the seed. The rose will eventually bloom with time, patience and practice.

Hurdle Three: I can be hit!

This is another one of those hurdles that looks kind of obvious from the outside. Well, of course you expect to be hit here. What did you think we were doing with this stick? She may even be able to tell you that she has no problems being hit with a stick.[25] We are, however, examining the thoughts that go on below the conscious process. The conflict between what she wants to believe and what the Lizard Brain tells her, in this case, is so great that it is one of the first places that she is likely to cry on the field. Admit it or not, my very unscientific personal survey suggests that over 75% of females have cried on the field, usually out of frustration and anger. Another release for the same frustration is uncontrolled giggling. Both reactions are somewhat disconcerting to the opponent but can be controlled with practice and understanding what is happening inside the head. This is one of the places that the stress created by the conflict of the Lizard Brain and the desire to fight often physically show up in an immediate release.

To understand the Lizard Brain's point of view, let's go back to the early years where the Lizard Brain learned. In male development, he is raised with contact games, wrestling in the

---

[25] When we describe the sport this way, we sound a little odd, don't you think?

living room, playing tag and the like. Every once and again he might get slapped on the hand in discipline or warning, but for the most part, physical combat has equated to friendship. As he grew he learned to greet other men with a firm hand shake, and if he was familiar with them a pat on the back or a chuck on the shoulder. You might even see grown men in a business environment greet each other with some friendly jockeying or some fake boxing. This adult behavior reinforces what his Lizard Brain learned young, most hitting is a way to show friendship and build relationships.

She in contrast was raised with the same occasional slap on the wrist or spank in warning or discipline, but if she played contact games she was called a Tom Boy. The next sentence was surely, "Don't worry, she'll grow out of it." This eventually became true, in some more than others. The lessons were reinforced as she grew. The school had no contact sports for women, there were no televised contact sports[26], and in the work place if a man shakes a woman's hand at all it is not the same handshake. Any more contact than the most basic handshake and someone is likely to file a sexual harassment suit somewhere.

In the course of a lifetime, about 95% of the time the average male has spent in contact with other people hitting, pushing, shoving, playing and so on, have been in friendly contact and comradely. About 95% of the time that the average female has spent in contact with others have been in discipline. It's not that she was disciplined more, just that the percentage to overall "hits" is greater. Overall she has been hit less, but of the times she has been hit, more of them have been in discipline and

---

[26] Women's boxing was not shown on TV until 1998. Title IX allowed that women would not be excluded based on sex, however they often don't make the male dominated team. And only 5% of high schools have female contact sport teams. As late as 2006 arguments and objections were still being heard by those higher education institutions that did not want to implement 'equal' female sports activities.

usually when she was younger (when the Lizard Brain remembers best). So, He and She go to the field to fight for the first time. He gets slapped up side the head with a stick and he thinks "Wow! A new game! New friends!", she takes the same shot and the thought in her head is "I did something Wrong!" In a huge rush there is a feeling of Shame, Guilt, Humiliation, and without bidding, Tears. To make matters worse, she knows that her eyes are leaking and is afraid that the person she trusts and respects (her trainer) is not going to respect her, because she is crying. This fear, and sense of impending loss brings greater anguish and more tears and starts a bad downward cycle.

Sometime after you and I were about four or five, spankings did not really hurt anymore, it was more the association that spanking related to parental displeasure and the sense of shame and humiliation of doing something wrong. If you have doubts, just tell a five-year-old they are in trouble and "Wait till your father gets home." The water works start up right on the spot, you did not even touch him. But the association of shame is already there. When she gets hit, she is having that same association brought forward. It does not happen as much with men because they had some physical contact to balance out this early association. This Hurdle is created by frustration. She knows she is crying and can't help it. The frustration comes from a conversation she just had with her Lizard Brain, it went by so fast she did not even notice. It goes something like this:

"You've been hit! You've done something wrong."

"I did not do anything wrong. I'm fighting!"

"Oh no, you were hit, you've been bad. You should be ashamed!"

"I'm not bad, I'm fighting."

"Girls don't fight. You are shamed!"

"I'm fighting and I'm enjoying it!"

"Oh, I see, so you want to be hit. No one respects an abused women."

This is a conversation she is not going to win the first time and the release for the stress created by the conflict is tears, or sometimes giggling uncontrollably. Since she did not so much hear the conversation as feel it, she has no idea why her eyes are leaking, or why she can't stop giggling, she just is, and she can't make it stop. If tears happen to be the release that you have experienced, do not worry, it could just have easily been giggles.[27] It is a natural release for stress. Everyone releases stress.

Some of the typical reactions trainers have to her release for stress are to tell her to stop giggling, laughing, crying or whatever. Well, she would like to, but can't. Telling her to stop will often increases the stress because she can not do what her trainer is asking her to do. She does not want to loose the trainer's respect and she will honestly try, but what she does not understand she cannot control and the stress continues. The trainer may think she is not serious, she is, and that is what produced the conflict that created the giggles in the first place. The trainer may feel like a heel because he made her cry. After all, he too has a Lizard Brain, and his says that he should not make her cry. For the trainer, be assured that you did not cause the tears, she is not weak, and she really does what to learn what you are showing. The tears like the giggles are a reflection of her honest desire to learn what is being shown, to fight when her entire upbringing says it is not proper.

For the trainer:

---

[27] My personal favorite is giggles, although I've done both. I discovered the giggles as a stress relief in Somalia. Trust me when I say it is very difficult to explain what you did to evade an ambush to a superior officer, while giggling.

Now that you know what causes the giggles or tears you have the ammo to solve the problem. First, convince yourself that you are not the cause of the tears. Yes, she is crying because you are fighting with her, but you did not create the conflict, the Lizard Brain did. Remind yourself that the tears or giggles are a reflection of how much she wants to learn this and how much she has trusted you to help her overcome her conditioning. If she is crying or giggling, give her a hug and laugh WITH her for a moment. Let her know that you still respect her and that this is a break through. The tears will likely turn to giggles. Explain the battle that is going on in her head and tell her that it is a good step forward. The fact that this stress shows up at all is a step to indicate that the Lizard Brain believes she is really serious about this.

Whatever you do, don't stop the practice. She still wants to fight. To walk away from the fight will reinforce the fear that you have lost respect for her. Worse yet, it lets the Lizard Brain win and he will have a stronger stand the next time. Do your best to ignore the tears, she is. Stop, explain what is going on, and continue with the lesson. If you can, turn it into a light hearted laugh at the absurdity of the conversation with the Lizard Brain. Most importantly, don't beat yourself up, this is a good thing. This hurdle will take some time to cross for most fighters, and even then will come back when she takes some time off from the sport. Have patience, she will overcome this obstacle as well.

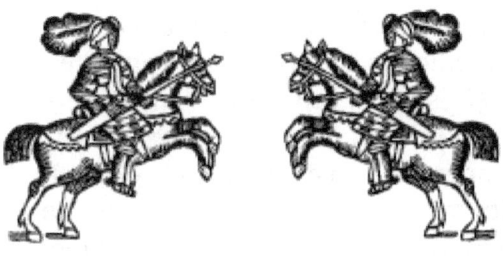

Hurdle Four: I can't do this, yet.

In every fighter's learning life there are things that do not come naturally. Let's face it, this is not the most natural sport there is. It might be a block, a blow, a stance, something that just does not work no matter how many times it is tried or how many ways it is explained. His answer to the frustration is – hit it harder. Her answer is often tears. This is not a reflection of being weak or unable to play the sport, it's a reflection of her frustration at not being able to do what she understands needs to be done.

Piled on top of the frustration of not having her body behave the way she would like, there is the fear that her trainer will not respect her because she has failed to do something. And even more insidious is the Lizard Brain response. *"See, I told you. You can't play this game. Here is proof. You've just been wasting your time. You haven't really been fighting, they are just playing with you."* These conditions make the simple act of not being able to do a new move almost devastating to her fighting. She might have leaky eyes again but this time, she will know that she is crying because she feels the frustration and sense of failure.

The sense of failure can often be created by the best intentions of the trainer to resolve the problem. Much of the frustration can simply be a communication problem. In communication there is a Sender, Receiver, Message and Transmission. Sometimes the

Transmission garbles the Message. Think of a cell phone or radio, the message is not always clear. Even when the Transmission method is simply voice to ear, the message gets confused when it is translated back by the Receiver. It is not the fault of either the Receiver or the Sender of the message, it is just a confused meaning. As an example, one of the first times I met this hurdle with my husband, he was showing me a particular blow/recovery/blow sequence. For the life of me, I just could not get it. I tried and tried and tried all evening.[28] At one point my husband, who loves and adores me, and would only think the best of me, in an effort to encourage me said "Don't worry, this is easy."

Most men will read this as "Don't worry, this is easy, with a little practice you will catch right on to it."

What most women hear is "This is easy. You must be as dumb as a rock if you can't do this."

The problem is that she can't do it, and the person she trusts the most to train her, the person who she respects, the person who she wants the respect of, just called her stupid. I stopped at the moment he said it and realized that I was hurt by his words, and knew that he would never deliberately hurt me. So I asked why he just called me stupid. He was shocked and surprised and desperately looked around the room for anyone that might have been using his voice when he was not paying attention. His reaction confirmed the suspicion that he had no idea that his words could be interpreted that way. So, the moral of the story is: What you say, may not be what the other person hears.

For the trainer:

---

[28] I later found out that, as a female, my bones don't allow me to move that way, but at the time I did not know this.

Stop. Explaining the same thing again will just make her feel like a rock, as in; "as thick as." Let her know that every fighter has some things that they don't catch on to right away. The best thing to do is tell her that you are not explaining it right. If you can, have someone else explain the movement. Take the blame as your own. After all you know how to do it, you're just not conveying it in such a way that she could understand it.

Keep in mind that language is a very tricky thing here. The words that leave your mouth are not necessarily the words that reach her ears. As an example say the sentence: "The lady hit the knight with the sword." Who has the sword, the knight or the lady? Was he hit with a sword, or was he holding the sword?

Another tactic is to explain that what you are showing is not easy. Tell her that you expect it to take her six months or more to master this sequence, you are just showing her how to do it now so that she sees that it is something to strive for. This is a challenge and her drive to please the trainer will have her doing this by next week. If she still has not been able to do it in a few weeks of trying, start looking for other reasons why it is not possible. Could it be a physical difference? Is there another movement that accomplishes the same result?

A fairly important concept to keep in mind at this point is that men and women tend to learn differently, particularly when it comes to physical conditioning. With a male student an effective training technique might involve targeting the same spot over and over again until he catches the block. There is a sense of pride that he has gotten the block, even if it is only one of ten times. He has a foot hold on the solution, and he will increase the percentages of success as he practices.

For her it is a bit of a different story. If she misses the block more than twice, the chances are she does not know how to do it. If the trainer keeps hitting the spot, as he would with a male student, she will often experience frustration and anger because he is "picking on her". From her perspective the trainer can see the weakness, knows what to do about it, but won't tell her. To top it off he keeps hitting her there – knowing that she can't block it. This creates huge amounts of frustration and anger, and gives the Lizard Brain more ammunition, and creates bruises she doesn't know how to stop. It's like playing a complex game that your opponent knows all the rules to, and you only know half. Show her the block. Go through it slow a few times and then work it into practice. His victory is in discovering the block for himself. Her victory is in successfully incorporating what she has been shown. Both will learn and remember the block effectively.

If all else fails put the concept aside for now. Even the best of fighters, male or female, have difficulty with some concepts. There will be something further down the road, maybe years from now that clicks into place and makes sense all of a sudden and this lesson that has been so difficult will be natural. The ground work that has been laid in this difficult period will come to benefit in the future. The important aspect of this lesson is to not let the Lizard Brain use it as a tangible tool to convince her not to fight.

Hurdle Five: Fighting outside the Comfort Zone

This is perhaps the most ingenious hurdle that the Lizard Brain has come up with in order to prevent her from breaking the mold of proper female activity. It is ingenious because it incorporates what we naturally have a tendency to do and expands it to the point of being detrimental.

We each like to measure ourselves and our skill. Watching a new fighter in this stage is almost amusing. They travel from event to event fighting in every practice and event they can get to for the sole purpose of finding out where they are on the grand pecking order of fighters. This seems to be a male dominated practice. Each up and coming wants to see how he measures up this week and does so by fighting the widest variety possible.

Women have a tendency to approach the same problem differently. They too want to know how much they are improving. Rather than measure it against others, they are more interested in knowing if they themselves have improved. For them the relative skill of someone else is not as important as what they have gained. To make this measure they try to use the same yardstick each time. They may fight their trainer, their squire brother, and their friend and consider it a great practice. Next week, the same people. The next week, once again the same three people. She is looking for an external measure of improvement for internal development. In some respect this is good. It really does not matter how much the other guys improve, we are each developing ourselves. This is where the Lizard Brain begins to use this tendency to its advantage.

At first this practice is a good thing, but when it becomes consistent, the Lizard Brain has taken over. It says "Fight only the people who know you are a girl. They will not hurt you. After all, you are not really fighting, girls don't do that, they are just playing with you. If you fight someone who does not know you are a girl, they might hurt you."

This hurdle shows up after she has reached some level of competency and is capable of expanding the depth and breadth of fighters she works with. Often she will not. This hurdle also explains the tendency for women to gladly fight a woman, but will be hesitant to fight a man they have never met.

For the trainer:

If you find yourself or your student in this hurdle there is a progressive direct solution. Choose a fighter who is competent, has nothing to prove, one who can scale a fight to a newer fighter and not fight at tournament level all the time. Suggest that she go fight him, take them over and introduce them. Watch the fight for the first few passes, and then leave to do something else. As the trainer you have done several things in this one action. You have shown that you believe that she is ready to move on. You have placed trust in her that she will not embarrass you. And most of all, you have moved her out of her "comfort zone". Only do it one fight a week for a while. Next week, suggest another fighter. By the time she has accumulated a dozen or so in her "comfort zone" she will come to realize that everyone is fighting her equally, that they are not going easy on her. It will reinforce the lesson that she is a fighter, just like anyone else out there.

If you have to take this step yourself, decide that you will fight one new fighter. Just one. Talk to them a bit first. Don't make excuses for you skill or apologize for your ability, just tell them you would like to fight someone that you have never fought before. Explain that you are open to instruction, and they will more than likely help the best they can.

Oddly enough, this is the one hurdle that is the most reoccurring. When she is out of fighting for a few months there will be a tendency to revert back to this stage. It is a comfort area, and fighting is emotionally uncomfortable for most women. She will want to find whatever she can to gain some measurement of emotional stability, and this is one of the places that it is easy to fall into a trap. A little of this is good, but too much of anything, including fighting inside a comfort zone can lead to delayed development of her skills.

Final Note on Hurdles

The hurdles that have been outlined may show up in larger or smaller degrees, depending on the student. While it has taken only a few pages to describe, categorize and suggest solutions to the problems, these solutions do not come easily. For many, these hurdles will be spaced years apart and take months to overcome once identified. To make matters harder, they have a tendency to come back if they are not constantly redressed and the solutions reinforced.

For some this creates a vicious cycle like:

    She does not fight because she is embarrassed

        - when she does not fight she does not get better

            – because she has not improved she thinks she can't fight

                – trying to do something she cannot makes her embarrassed.

Regular training and practice will overcome the hurdles in time. Don't expect it to happen all at once or suddenly. In many places pu͜͠͝͠ ͟͠͝͞ss the next hurdle will do more harm than good. They have been outlined here so that teacher and student can work on them one at a time and overcome them each in its own time. Of course if you are the student and have read this carefully, the back of your brain is already working on overcoming the objections of the Lizard Brain (Keep at it!).

The up side to these hurdles is that when she has successfully negotiated the obstacle course that the Lizard Brain has created, she is ready to walk on the field as an equal to any fighter out there. She will not experience some of the more difficult stages that male fighters pass through such as:

> ➤ The "Wild Fighter" who does not have control of the weapon or fight.

> ➤ She knows the discipline of working on the pell because she spent a longer time there when she was convincing herself that it was acceptable to hit people.

> ➤ She is less likely to lose her temper in a fight and do something she regrets, as she has already spent a great deal of time exploring and marshaling her emotions.

Some male students will see part of themselves in some of these hurdles. Gender is not the only thing that creates these hurdles, just a substantial contributor. It's not so much a matter of her being better or worse than her male counterpart, just that the developmental path that each takes is likely to be different.

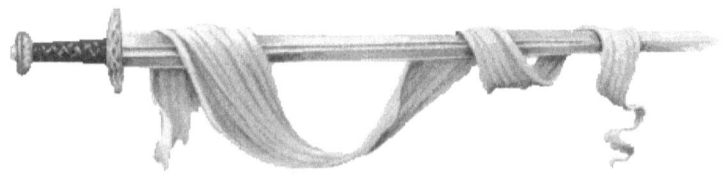

IV. Prejudices and Pondering

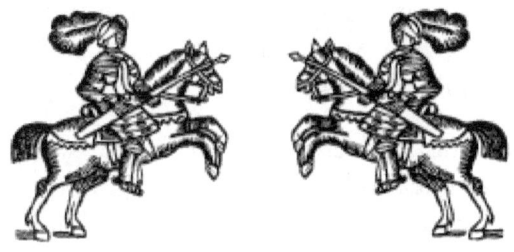

<u>Prejudices</u>

If you are reading this, I make the assumption that you are human. And like most humans you are naturally pre-judge your environment. Yes, experience adds to our learning, but much of our survival comes from our innate knowledge. We know that fire is harmful – certain sounds cue our 'fight or flee' senses. When we walk down the street and pass someone, we have pre-judged that person and determined it was safe to have our back to them. We did not stop the person and ask their life history to find out if they were likely to stab us in that back. We looked at the person, categorized them based on previous experience and determined that they were safe to pass – all within a moment or two.

There is a great public service announcement that airs on TV every once and again. It is a commercial in black and white showing a profile view of a bald black man in his early thirties, the wall behind him has horizontal lines that might be used as height markers, it looks like a mug shot. As the man's face is slowly rotated to the frontal view the voice over starts to read the rap sheet as it is printing on the screen next to the man. "Joseph Gardner, first conviction at age 16, convicted grand larceny, breaking and entering, armed robbery, assault with a deadly weapon, wanted for murder, rape and arson. Arrested by officer

Denise Howard – Pictured here." The commercial illustrates that we use prejudice in our everyday life. The question is not "Are we prejudice?" but, "Do we extend our natural prejudice to the level of being socially unacceptable?".

It is unfortunate, but the average female fighter will come across some form of prejudice in her fighting career. In the '70s female fighters wore colored green sashes on the war field and men who would not fight women wore purple sashes signifying they agreed simply not to fight each other. At one time in this sport there were men who deliberately fought to hurt women. The fact that we find this behavior reprehensible today indicates that we no longer allow this to be acceptable conduct. Chauvinism has evolved from a prejudice to a socially unacceptable form of discrimination, culturally as well as in the SCA. Even today there are those accomplished fighters who refuse to fight an opponent simply because she is female. When a person defines themselves by their gender rather than their ability or accomplishment they become threatened when the definition of that gender is endangered. Although it is not seen as much today, a woman who defines herself in her gender would be appalled to do work outside the home, change a tire or mow the lawn. A man might see his gender as suited for hard labor, military service, and fighting. For these people there are clearly defined gender roles, he fixes the car, she buys the groceries. When someone chooses to cross these boundaries a conflict arises. When this conflict occurs on the field both he and she must reconcile their beliefs with the situation before them. This may show up in some unfortunate behavior. The reconciliation may take the form of calibration differences when taking blows, or striking her with a blow he would never give his male friend, both, or by refusing to fight her at all. She reconciled her beliefs in order to get to the field to begin with. One of the most absurd things I've come across is the opponent or trainer that feels justified to hit her harder or treats her worse in training because "She is just going to quit anyway, so might as well make her do it sooner." I was a little stunned that the gent really did not see his contribution to making her quit.

If you experience this gender bias, realize that not all people are slaves to beliefs. Trust that you can go out and find someone who is not. If you see a female fighter become subject to such behavior, stop it if you can, or offer yourself as a contrast. Many of the feelings of camaraderie and belonging dissolve when this behavior appears. Some men reading this will not have a frame of reference for this phenomenon. It is difficult to describe, but imagine someone refusing to fight you because you lived on the other side of town, and they believe people who live there are not worthy of fighting. You like where you live, and see nothing wrong with it, but somehow, you are less than acceptable in that person's eyes.

There are also a variety of subtle actions that can add up to create obstacles. Women who show up at a practice with a male companion may not be presented with the opportunity to learn about fighting, where he is automatically accepted. Oddly, if she shows up unattached there are plenty of men to talk to her about fighting. She may likely train three times as long before she is approached about being a squire. She is often not given the opportunity to warm up as are male fighters prior to fighting. After a pregnancy, and a year off, she may be asked to re-authorize where a man with a year off is not. In training, most men feel compelled to train her, even if she is a more competent fighter.

This last one is one of those subtle though annoying prejudices. If every fighter can be ranked on a scale of 1-10, 1 being brand new and 10 an accomplished Crown winner, seven or so is a knight, a number three male will still not feel comfortable teaching a number one male. It is not until they start to get to the number four stage that they might feel qualified to teach a number one male fighter. In short, they feel comfortable teaching two or three levels below their ability. In contrast, that same number three male will feel perfectly competent to teach a female ranked one to six. Even if she is clearly a better fighter, there is something in many men that refuses to see this and, with every good intention, he attempts to instruct her on the "right" way to do something. I've been fighting for over 25 years and I would be rich if I had a nickel for every time a new fighter tried teaching me a flat snap even today. If you are the victim of this prejudice, smile and thank him anyway, he does mean well, he too has a Lizard Brain, one that is telling him he must help women. Each of these instances happens often. The male reader may never have noticed it before, but she did.

Some of these things may seem small and insignificant to the male reader. In truth, any single item surely could be brushed off and considered an annoying incident. Keep in mind though that she sees it every day, at work, school and now on the field. She may now see things as prejudice that are not meant to be prejudice. She is likely to be very sensitive to the issue. She is used to defending her choice to fight to her Lizard Brain, family, self and friends. For him: If you get snapped at by a woman, for what seems to be an innocuous comment, you may have a better idea of what produced what at first glance seems to be an unreasonable reaction. Find out what words exactly produced the reaction; you may have said something that was understood differently than you meant it. For her: If you find yourself snapping at someone for a perceived insult, stop and ask yourself why he said it, what does he not know that you do? What in his upbringing makes him believe the way he does? Would he have said the same thing to a male student, and you have just taken it badly? Paraphrase what you think you heard and ask him if that is what he meant. Sometimes people are remarkably surprised to hear how someone else can interpret their own words. Remember that the words that left his mouth may not be the words that reached your ears.

Choosing a Trainer

Choosing a trainer is not done lightly. If you are that instructor, you may not realize how much she has just invested in you. The person who teaches a female fighter is entrusted with helping her overcome the social conditioning that she was raised with. She is asking that person to help break her from the mold she has of herself. She has trusted the person with the very definition of herself. She respects and wants the respect of her trainer. The teacher must be close enough to be trusted, and removed enough to be railed against in moments of frustration. The challenge for the trainer is to remove gender from the relationship, but not the lesson.

For some, it is possible to have a husband teach a wife. The most successful cases of this come from a man who already knows how to fight and is fairly competent. He must also be willing to teach her on the field, and see her as an equal as soon as they are off the field. These cases are rare, but they do exist. In order for this arrangement to work, she has to be absolutely convinced that he loves her. She has to be able to take criticism from him. He has to be able to trust her when she says it does not work, even though it works for any number of male students. I would not recommend that this arrangement be tried unless he has had several students in the past and is considered a good teacher and very competent fighter to begin with. In short, it is possible, but there be dragons in these waters. *Besides, the couch is NOT comfortable and the doghouse is already occupied.* (Note from His Grace.)

There are some other warnings that the prospective female student must acknowledge and be on the lookout for. Because that trainer is in such a position of trust, it is easy for him to take advantage of it. There are instances of trainers using the position to gain a bed partner. He is able to do this because of the respect, admiration, trust and desire to please that comes in the package. There is a reason that Psychologists, Teachers and Policemen who do this are put in jail. It is a violation of the teacher student relationship. If you find yourself falling in love, change trainers. If it is love the feeling will not go away and your fighting will not suffer. If it is idealization on your part, you will see it when you switch. If it is an abuse of power on his part, he will do everything he can to keep you from changing trainers and will want nothing more to do with you when you have.

There is one last word of warning. Being a squire is to some a great honor, but be careful of the knight who asks. Find out what they think of females fighting and why they want to train you. As a prominent Duke has explained more than once, there are those out there who take females squires in order to be politically correct. They have no intention of training them and will find any excuse not to. This can have a devastating effect on her fighting. Now she does not believe herself good enough to fight with her knight, and is already spoken for so she is less likely to be approached by those who would be willing to teach her. This isn't to say you should not accept the offer from a knight who approaches you. It is to say, do research. Don't let the excitement and thrill prevent you from doing some research on the person. If he is honest, he won't mind, in fact, he will probably be happy that you are taking it seriously.

Make the choices about teachers carefully. The obstacles of distance can be overcome when the benefits of a good match between teacher and student can be found. Take your time, and make sure the relationship is a good one. It is much more difficult to break a relationship than make one, and all sorts of damage can be done in between.

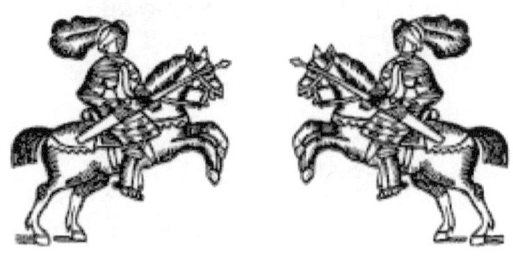

<u>Why does she fight?</u>

There are as many reasons to fight as there are people fighting. On the surface she might say, because it is fun. This is a fairly safe answer, and one that most people would understand and few would go beyond. This answer, however, usually just satisfies the questioner and has little to do with the reality of what brought her to the field.

Some women fight, or attempt to, in order to boyfriend shop. You know you have seen them. They often have a full set of make up and a fresh manicure before going to practice. They are the ones who wrinkle the nose and gingerly put on the helmet as if walking into a dark room. They often hang out with the fighter crowd and explain that they want to fight but spend most of the time talking with the gals rather than watching the fighting. This type of boyfriend shopping is helpful when looking for an attentive and patient partner. If she is shopping, she will not fight. (The problem is that many of the symptoms of the hurdles of an earnest female fighter are also the symptoms of the **Shopper**.) You will know the difference when she is more interested in learning to fight than she is in a particular person.

Some women fight for the attention. **The Attention Seeker** is sometimes seen as a sub set of the Shopper. This is a male dominated sport and a female fighting is a novelty. There is often a great deal of attention for the new female fighter. If this is her only motivation, she eventually will tire of it and move on to something else.

Some women fight out of obligation. The **Obligated Fighter** might be part of a fighting household and it is their way to contribute to the unit. They might have been made a squire and fight because it is what their knight expects There is the potential for her to eventually fight because she wants to, but for now, she fights because another wants her to.

Some women fight to be accepted by the guys. This is not unusual. Many are looking for the sense of camaraderie and belonging that are present among fighters. Most women grew up without that "team" concept, and find that it is achievable here. On of the dangers in this motivation is the concept that she can only be a "dress lady" or a "fighter lady". In order to fit in she may take up more than just the fighting. She may dress as the men do, tell crude jokes if they do, and try to be **One of the Guys**. A real guys guy. This can spring up from not knowing that she can be both a lady and a fighter and that she does not need to choose one over the other. Once, while giving a lecture on women and fighting I was running late and had been fighting a little to long on the field. I came to class still in armor, hot and sweaty. A friend who knew that the class I was teaching was not meant to be done in armor, quickly picked up my dress, toiletry bag, a friend and a cloak. They held up a screen in the corner of the room while I talked and changed clothes. In six minutes fifty two seconds I was back in a dress, hair done and jewelry in place. *(I confess, I've had practice)* .The lesson here is simple: She dresses how she chooses to dress. She behaves the way she chooses to behave. Fighting is not an excuse to dress like a guy, use foul language, belch with the boys, or scratch genitals in public. If she chooses to do those things, that is a separate choice. Frankly, fighting is not an excuse for guys to do this either, it is just choice.

The **War Fighter** is a common form of the female fighter species. This is the one who fights only in wars. She may even excel here, and show no interest in fighting on the tourney field. This may come from the feeling that war fighting gives her everything she wants. She gets the sense of team, belonging, and does not take up her entire event time fighting. She satisfies her need to contribute to the whole and be a part of a winning team. Many women start out as support, move to light fighting and may even eventually go to heavy combat. War fighting speaks to that part of her that is defending the home front. When she is ready, the stepping stone from the War Fighter to the Tourney Fighter will be when she moves from defensive positions, such as a shield wall, to the offensive positions, such as pike or glave, or into a skirmish unit.

The **Future Knight in Training** is characterized by a love for all forms of fighting, a desire to learn, and patience with herself and those who train her. She is the one who experiences a setback (and they will be there) but does not let it stop her from trying again. She has a determination to learn, play, enjoy and grow in the sport. She is the one who learns not to be defined by others limitations. A fighter in any of the other categories can develop into this stage, when she so chooses. You will know this fighter because she takes the field ready to learn. Faced with an obstacle she defines it and works to overcome it. She does not attempt to hide her gender by behaving as one of the boys, she is proud of who and what she is. She knows that she is improving, and takes steps to insure that she does so every day. She is prepared to be treated as an equal, if not the same. You can look to find this person knighted some day.

IV. Practical

Blows and Blocks

The following pages consist of mini-movies on fighting. To make the mini-movie gather the first ten pages of pictures and keep your eye on either the top, middle or bottom set as you flip through the pages. There are three movements on each set of ten pages. The next series of movements is on the back of the first ten pages – always flip toward the back of the book. The motions shown here show the female form for each of the blows. In some cases there are no differences between the female and the male form, in some the differences are small but significant. Use these photos as a starting place. There are many ways to do the same shot, practice, and use what works for you and your body. We can not go over everything in this section. We will not discuss sword retrieval or shot set up or any of the other things that make up the slight nuances of the game. Those are best learned one on one with an excellent teacher. This is just a start. The key will be to throw the blow without feeling an uncomfortable jarring sensation in the knee, wrist, back or arm……or anywhere else actually.

After you have read the explanation and flipped through the mini-movie, or reviewed the sequence pictures in the electronic form, on a shot, flip through it a few more times and look at the block.

The secrete to blocking is economy of motion. The less the shield moves, the less energy you expend, the less tired you are and the longer you can play. There are exceptions to even this rule, but in the beginning keep the shield close to the body and the blocks as minimal as possible.

First Set: Onside Shots
1. Upper Right – Flat Snap, Head
2. Middle Right – Flat Snap, Body
Lower Right – Flat Snap, Leg
On the back of the pages:
Upper Left – Low Wrap
Middle Left – Rising Wrap
Lower Left – Inside Leg

Second Set: Offside and Center Shots
Upper Right - Offside Head
Middle Right – Offside Body
Lower Right – Offside Leg
Upper Left – Overhead Wrap
Middle Left – Centerline Shot
Lower Left – Sweep Through, Offside Body

Third Set: Combinations
Upper Right – Rick Rack
Middle Right – Snap and Wrap
Lower Right – Onside/Offside
Upper Left – Leg Fake
Middle Left – J shot
Lower Left – Shield Press/Offside

1. <u>The Flat Snap to the Head</u>

The first sequence starting in the upper right hand side of this page and continuing on for the next ten pages is the **Flat Snap to the Head**. It may be best to practice this shot without the sword in hand first. Stand up straight, weight evenly distributed between your feet in the beginning stance. Visualize a line from the top of your head through the center of your body and down to the ground between your legs. The starting point for the body will have the hips and shoulders facing the opponent with the sword on the shoulder and the pommel facing the target. (When the blow is finished the side of the hip and shoulder will be facing the opponent.) The blow begins with the sword hand at or near the

Flat Snap to Head

Flat Snap to Body

Flat Snap to Leg

Low Wrap

Rising Wrap

Inside Leg

2. Low Wrap

The **Low Wrap** is sometimes called a **Butt Wrap** depending on exactly where it lands. This particular shot seems to be easier for many women than it is for most men. This may be that the tendons in the arm and shoulder naturally flex in this motion. Just as any shot, however, it will require practice. Start with the hand on the shoulder as with the previous blows. The hips, shoulders and body turn just as before up to the point where the hand starts to move away from the shoulder. Remember the analogy of the waiter serving soup? Imagine the bowl of soup again and this time you are going to dump it in the customer's lap.

Flat Snap continued:

shoulder with the palm up. Imagine holding a bowl of soup like a waiter. Rotate the body, hips and shoulders moving together, around your centerline. Imagine smelling the soup as you pass it by your nose. When the rotation is about half way through, the hand starts to move away from the shoulder. You have essentially launched your hand from your shoulder. The body continues to rotate and the hand moves forward toward the target. The sword swings around picking up speed as your hand leaves your shoulder. Just before impact tighten the back leg and push a little with the back foot to give the leading hip a small push. (It's much like the hip pop a belly dancer does.) When the timing is correct the impact of the sword and the hip push happen at the same moment.

Flat Snap to Head

Flat Snap to Body

Flat Snap to Leg

| Blows and Blocks 105

Low Wrap

Rising Wrap

Inside Leg

As the hand moves away from the shoulder guide your hand (and basket hilt) toward the level of the opponent's hip and begin to turn your hand over so the palm is facing to the inside. Just as you reach full extension several things must come together at once. 1) The wrist continues to rotate and 'dump the bowl of soup' until the palm is face down, 2) The shove from the back foot is completed at the moment of impact and, 3) Your arm must not be locked straight at the instant the blow hits, you can, but it will eventually lead to tendon damage. A wrap shot is mostly a matter of great timing. There are several ways to do the same shot. A second way is to start the shot identically, however, at the split second before impact push with the lead foot and force your hips back, counter to the direction they were turning.

Flat Snap continued:

In the finished position your head is turned to the side looking down your shoulder and your hand is lined up under your opponent's nose (for a man shoulder elbow and hand are lined up with the opponents opposite shoulder). Your shoulders and hips are in alignment with each other, your back is straight and the weight evenly distributed between your feet. Your lead knee and toes are facing the opponent. Practice timing in this shot to push the hip just at the moment of impact. Allow the sword to be an extension of your own reach.

Some of the common variations include changing the starting position by showing presenting the pommel toward the opponent, or putting the sword blade down the back or even bringing the blade up and moving the hilt further forward.

Flat Snap to Head

Flat Snap to Body

Flat Snap to Leg

| Blows and Blocks 107

Low Wrap

Rising Wrap

Inside Leg

This sharp pull sets up a whip effect at the tip of the sword and drives the tip of the sword in quickly to the target.

This shot is one of the ones to be careful about placing. Do not use the shot without practicing the placement, slowly and consistently. If this shot is delivered with too much enthusiasm or not enough control it is easy to over rotate the wrist so that the palm is facing out. This variation is only a fraction of an inch at your hand, but at the end of the sword the error is compounded. The tip of the sword will turn down and likely hit at or below the knee behind the opponent. This is a spot that is next to impossible to armor and is considered an illegal target. With the speed that this shot can come in it is likely to cause some pain and damage. Instead of being impressed with what you learned, those around

Flat Snap continued:

The shot is a basic for most fighters and can be delivered very quickly with practice. Keep in mind that "basic" does not mean "easy".

Flat Snap to Head

Flat Snap to Body

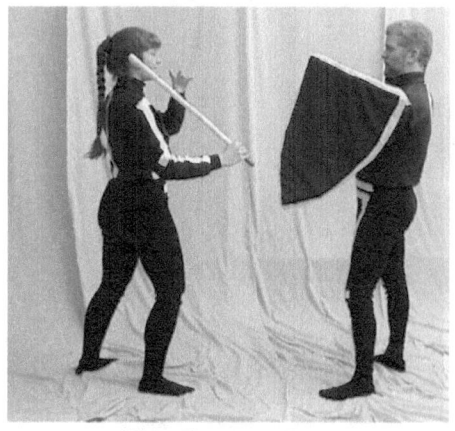

Flat Snap to Leg

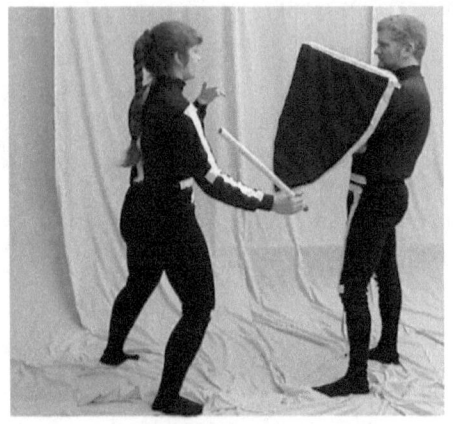

Low Wrap

Rising Wrap

Inside Leg

you will be upset with the lack of control. Practice, slow and precise first.

3. <u>Flat Snap to the Body</u>

The second shot, shown here in the middle of the page (for the paper copy) is **the Snap to the Body**. The motion is very similar to the Snap to the Head, just a different ending target. Start again with your hips and shoulders facing your opponent, sword on your shoulder with the pommel facing your target. Begin the rotation of the body hips and shoulders as a unit. At about the half way mark again, start to move your hand away from your body. The hand continues on toward the target and your body continues to move around your centerline. This time, instead of serving the bowl of soup to the person's nose, serve it to mid body.

Flat Snap to Head

Flat Snap to Body

Flat Snap to Leg

| Blows and Blocks 111

4. Rising Wrap

Low Wrap

Rising Wrap

Inside Leg

The **Rising Wrap** is much like the Low Wrap. In this shot the look of the blow is identical up until very nearly the last fraction of a second before impact. The blow starts, as all the blows so far, with the hand on the shoulder, palm up in the' waiter holding a bowl of soup pose'. Body, shoulders, and hips turn, halfway through the hand moves away from the body and down toward the leg. As the arm reaches extension the wrist begins to turn over to 'dump the bowl of soup'.

Just as in the first snap shot, push with the back foot and "pop" with the hip just before contact. When the blow is delivered the side of your body will be facing toward the target, your arm extended but not straight (never lock the elbow), and your body weight evenly distributed between your feet.

Practice this and all blows slowly at first. Try the motion with an empty hand first. When the motion is smooth try the blow with a stick in your hand. When timing and motion are correct, move up to using a sword.

Flat Snap to Head

Flat Snap to Body

Flat Snap to Leg

Low Wrap

Rising Wrap

Inside Leg

When the arm is extended and the palm facing inward, as if you were getting ready to shake someone's hand, slightly change the rotation of the wrist. Instead of continuing in the direction you are going and turning the hand palm down, as in the Low Wrap, bend your wrist back toward you raising the tip of the sword. The basket hilt stays in more or less the same position. The tip of the sword should rise and strike above the waist. With practice this shot can land anywhere you want between the waist and head. One of the wonderful things about this shot is that it looks just like the one that is targeting the leg. If the opponent believes that you are targeting the leg, the leg is what they will protect. When the leg is covered, the head is open.

You are in a Race

Do the motions slowly and accurately first. Speed will come later. You are in a race with Speed and Accuracy. Speed is trying to catch you while you are trying to catch Accuracy. If Speed catches you first, you will never catch Accuracy with Speed on your back. Work on accuracy first, speed will come.

Flat Snap to Head

Flat Snap to Body

Flat Snap to Leg

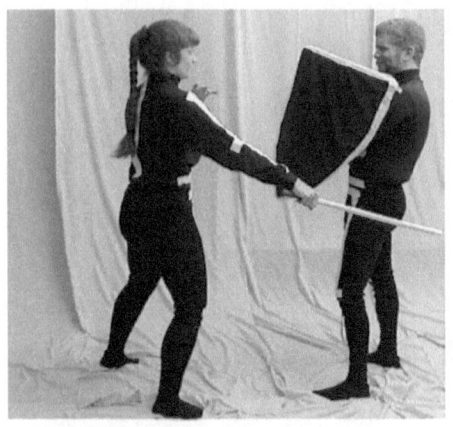
Low Wrap

Rising Wrap

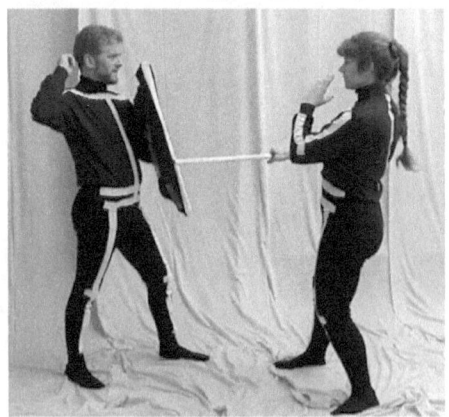
Inside Leg

All to many students make the mistake of throwing blows fast at first. Speed is not everything. Speed without control is dangerous. Speed without the proper transfer of power is ineffective. It is very difficult to develop precision at full speed. Practice precision, practice balance, practice the 'pop' with the hip that gives the extra punch in a shot. Let speed come on its own when you know the move so well that you can do it with your eyes closed, and hit the same mark every time, even when you are moving around. Speed will find you. You must find precision first.

5. <u>Snap to the Leg</u>

Just as the Snap to the Body, the **Snap to the Leg** is done with similar motions to the basic Snap. This time when your body has turned about half way and the hand starts to move away from your shoulder throw the blow to the mid thigh. This shot is particularly useful when the opponent has a tendency to lift the shield a little too high.

Flat Snap to Head

Flat Snap to Body

Flat Snap to Leg

| Blows and Blocks

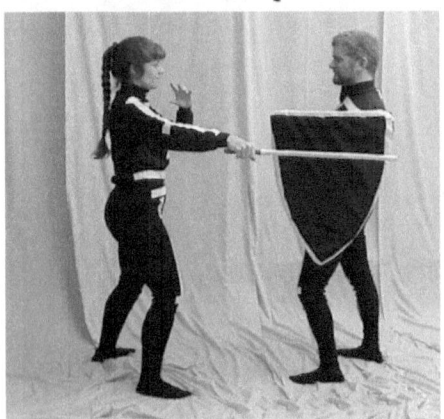

Low Wrap

Rising Wrap

Inside Leg

6. <u>Inside Leg</u>

The **Inside Leg** shot will be the first blow discussed that is not "on side". This term refers to the side closest to your sword, usually covered by their shield. The Inside Leg shot still attacks the shield side leg, but it does so by moving inside the shield. Before working on this shot make sure you have the hip rotation described in the Low Wrap where the hips move back to the starting point after rotating to the side, providing the pop that whips the sword into the target. When you are confident with this counter hip rotation try this shot.

Each of the Snap shots starts out very much the same, so the opponent will not be able to tell where the shot is going to land until after your hand starts to move away from your body. Mix it up a little. If you have thrown several shots in a row to the head, throw one at the leg. Better yet, throw several to the leg first and surprise them with a killing blow to the head.

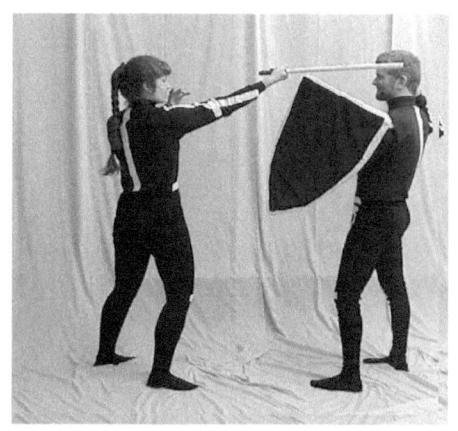

Flat Snap to Head

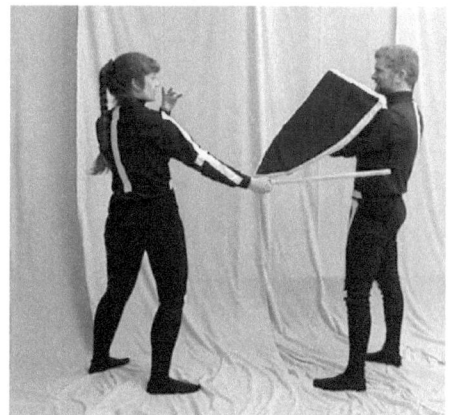

Flat Snap to Body

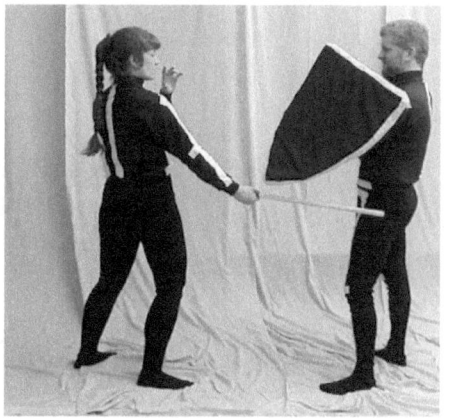

Flat Snap to Leg

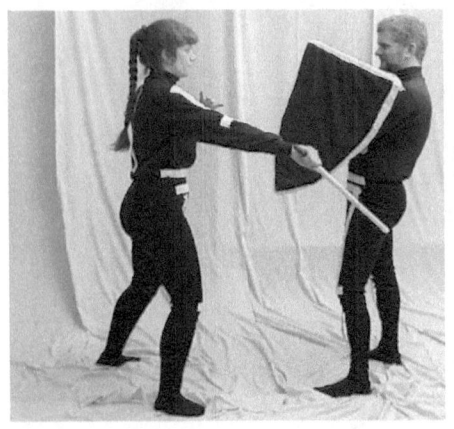

Low Wrap

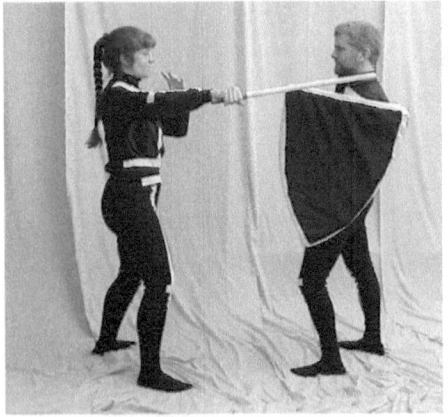

Rising Wrap

Inside Leg

Start in the basic position, bowl of soup on the shoulder, hips and shoulders facing the opponent. Start the rotation, hips, shoulders and body all together. When the hand comes away from the shoulder this time, move the hand as if you were going to do a Flat Snap, but do not extend the arm. At this point you should be looking at the inside of your wrist with your palm facing skyward, and your arm bent. Now, turn your palm over, dumping the bowl of soup and counter rotate the hips and shoulders. Allow the tip of the sword to make a ¾ circle turn in front of you to land on the inside of the opponents leg. The timing is right when the tip of the sword hits the inside of the 'on side leg, at the same time that the hips and shoulders return to the squared up starting position. Precision is required to prevent from hitting a knee.

> Timing a blow is the secret to powerful hitting.
>
> - Bruce Lee

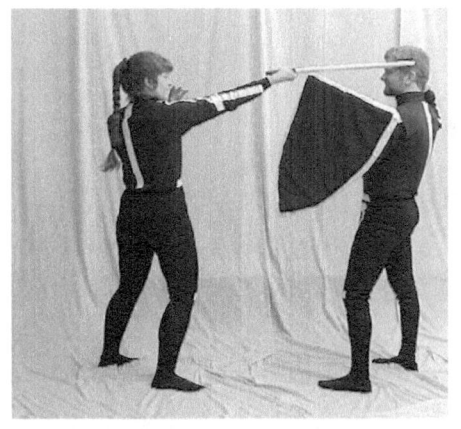
Flat Snap to Head

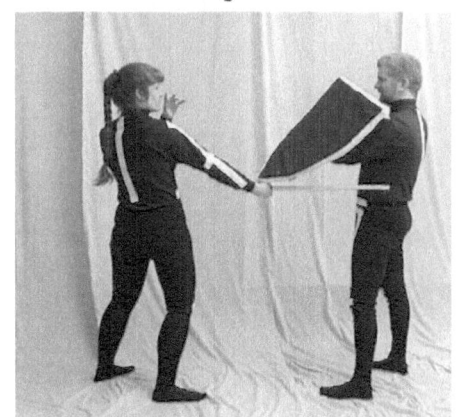
Flat Snap to Body

Flat Snap to Leg

Low Wrap

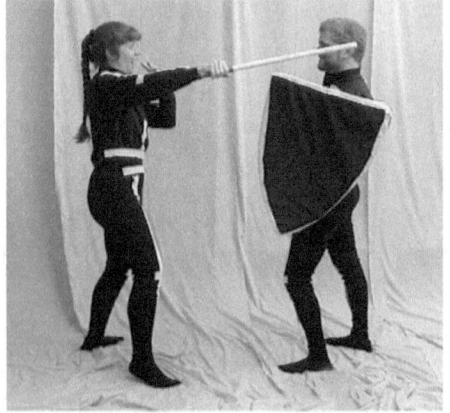
Rising Wrap

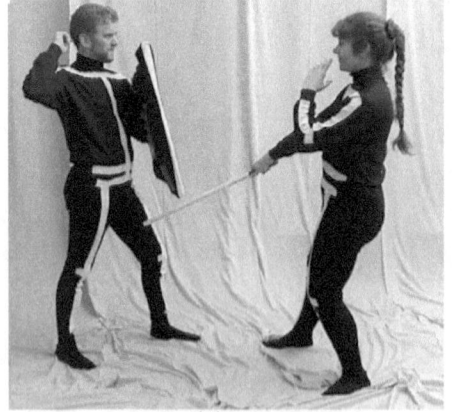
Inside Leg

While apologizing when you hit someone correctly is an indicator of Hurdle Two, apologizing when you hit someone incorrectly is an indicator of good etiquette. Everyone misses a shot and has one land badly on occasion. The key is to know when you landed the shot poorly and take responsibility for doing so. If you remain quiet in the face of errors the assumption will be that you did not know that you hit an illegal target, or worse yet, that you meant to.

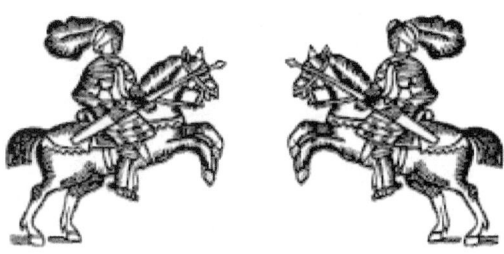

Second Set: Offside and Center Shots

Upper Right - Offside Head

Middle Right – Offside Body

Lower Right – Offside Leg

Upper Left – Overhead Wrap

Middle Left – Centerline Shot

Lower Left – Sweep Through, Offside Body

7. Offside Head:

The 'Offside' shots, as you may have already surmised are the blows that attack the side opposite your sword side, usually the opponent's sword side (for right handed fighters). The good part is that your opponent is more open on the sword side, the down side is that it is harder to get to. This blow begins by pushing up the sword while the blade is still mostly behind the head. The sword arm crosses up and over your head, as if you were taking that bowl of soup an raising it up and out of the way. Once the sword hand is above the head begin to bring the blade from behind you to the front.

Offside Head

Offside Body

Offside Leg

8. <u>Overhead Wrap</u>

This blow begins as all others have in the basic position. This time the hand is pushed up just as in the offside shots, but push up just as far as you can without spilling the 'bowl of soup'. This time, instead of the sword moving around your head, the sword tip comes straight over the top of the head. There will come a moment when the sword is straight up in the air and the palm of your hand will be facing your opponent. As the momentum of your sword carries the blade toward you opponent, rotate your wrist with emphasis and 'dump the soup'.

Overhead Wrap

Centerline Shot

Sweep Through Off Side Body

If you practice this a great deal out of armor it may take some readjustment when you do it in armor as the top of the helm is likely to be a few inches higher than your head. Keep the sword hand where it is and allow the momentum of the blade to move forward over your head and shield. As the blade begins to move to the inside of the opponents shield shift your weight to the back foot and lean to that side while flicking the wrist toward the opponents head. Imagine flinging water off you hand to get the 'flick' motion. In this demonstration, the target has not attempted to block, most however will. This is one of those places where the extra few degrees of angle will offer an advantage for the female fighter.

Offside Head

Offside Body

Offside Leg

Overhead Wrap

Centerline Shot

Sweep Through Off Side Body

Your hand will end with your palm facing outward, thumb pointed down and the back of your blade on the target. It is not important to be taller than your target, you only need your hand to be higher than the opponent's shield in order for this shot to work. Keep the hand and wrist as close to the top of the opponent's shield as possible. The blow gains a bit of extra speed –read power- with the wrist rotation at the end.

Because women are naturally more flexible than men, this shot may seem a little easier for the female student. This one requires great timing, but it also requires the flexibility to turn the palm out and the thumb down in the final stage of this shot.

This shot can be very fast and difficult to predict for the opponent, in addition most experienced fighters will block the minimum possible in order to conserve energy. Because the final 'flick' of the hand for a female tends to be a few extra degrees more than the comparable man, the shot lands just a little farther inside when she throws the blow. As a result, he will often think he has blocked the shot and he will still hear a tell tale 'tink' that tells him that he was hit in the eyes. The lean at the end helps accentuate this angle advantage.

In this blow, as in many others, the last fraction of a second of the shot is the most important. It is at this moment that the power generated by the momentum of the sword is transferred to the target.

Offside Head

Offside Body

Offside Leg

Overhead Wrap

Centerline Shot

Sweep Through Off Side Body

9. Centerline Shot

This shot is often called a hammer shot. This is the movement in its most basic form. The hand moves from the shoulder to the waist and the momentum of the sword brings the power to the target. Imagine hitting a nail at waist level with a hammer. This shot can be very fast and is often used when the opponent allows his shield to drift away from protecting the center line of the body. This is also called a Slot Shot as it often fits into the narrow opening made by someone pulling their shield to the side to take a look at you.

By flicking the wrist, the tip of the sword moves even faster than it did when the blow closed the distance between you and the opponent. Energy is described by modern physics as $E=Mc^2$. This is translated to Energy = Mass x Acceleration^2. There are two ways to increase Energy, or what you are putting into the blow. You can increase the weight of the sword, the mass, or you can increase the speed of the blow. Because Acceleration is squared in this formula, energy, or power, is increased more by speed than by weight of the weapon. The faster the blow lands, the harder it hits.

Keep in mind though that speed will do you no good if you do not develop the precision to place the shot first.

Offside Head

Offside Body

Offside Leg

Overhead Wrap

Centerline Shot

Sweep Through Off Side Body

Each of these demonstrations starts with the sword straight down the back. The sword does not need to start there, this is just for demonstration. The sword will naturally have a place to return to when you are resting between combinations. In this case, that resting place is on the model's shoulder with the sword down the back. Some teachers prefer to see the sword sticking straight out behind with the pommel facing the opponent, others with the sword already straight up in the air or pointing at the ground behind them. I don't recommend the last two for newer fighters as it is very difficult to generate power in this position. For now, rest the sword on your shoulder and learn each shot from the same starting position. Later on you will use drills to smoothly transition from one blow to the next.

10. Offside Body

The next offside shot is to the body. This shot like the previous one, is best done with a little movement. The opponent may be trying to move past you or you may have to move to the side to create the opening. Either way, the movement helps open up the offside a little more than it might have been otherwise. This blow starts the same as the previous one with a push upward with the sword hilt to clear your head. Swing the tip of the sword over and around your head.

Offside Head

Offside Body

Offside Leg

11. <u>Sweep through, Off Side Body</u>

Overhead Wrap

Centerline Shot

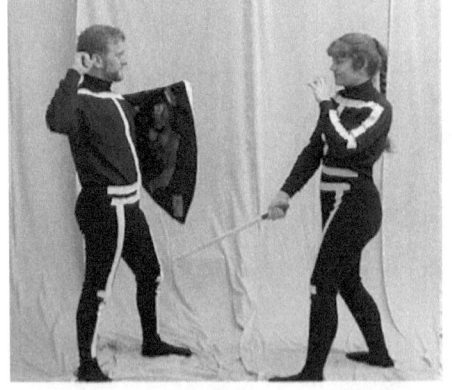

Sweep Through Off Side Body

This shot starts with a deception to the opponent, called a fake. The first part of the blow looks just like the Leg Wrap. In fact, you really want them to believe that this really is going to be a great wrap to the leg or butt. Instead of letting the tip of the sword wrap around to the back of the opponents leg, miss the shot, draw it short, and let the sword sweep between the two of you. Let the momentum of the sword 'wind you up'. As your opponent goes to block the leg shot, they are likely to expose the other hip.

When the sword is between you and your opponent, step to the side and forward about 45 degrees with your shield foot (the description is for a right handed person, turn it around for the lefty). This motion helps move the opponent out of a protective position behind the shield. Complete the blow with the flick of the wrist while landing the sword in the body. The timing becomes critical to make sure both feet are firmly planted on the ground when the blow lands.

Offside Head

Offside Body

Offside Leg

Overhead Wrap

Centerline Shot

Sweep Through Off Side Body

Hold the sword parallel to the ground, tighten the arm and wrist and rotate your whole body, landing the sword on the exposed hip. Again, this shot is shown with the shield foot forward for variety sake. Try it both ways. This blow can hit hard because of the whipping action when changing directions with the sword. Don't shy away from the hard blow, just be aware and adjust as necessary.

In this example we have started to 'create' openings. The opening was not there when you started the blow. In fact, the opening only showed up in reaction to your first movements. This and many of the remaining shots are intermediate movements and require more timing and precision and practice.

Keep in mind the earlier lesson about hips and shoulders. They must be in line with the center of the body and both feet on the ground in order to get the best transfer of power, at the moment of impact. Your feet can be airborne a fraction of a second before or after impact, but for the best power they need to be on the ground when you strike.

Offside Head

Offside Body

Offside Leg

Overhead Wrap

Centerline Shot

Sweep Through Off Side Body

> If we know the path of the sword well, we can wield it easily.
>
> -Miyamoto Musashi

12. <u>Offside Leg</u>

This blow, as well as # 12, is shown with the shield foot forward. It's not that they can not be effectively thrown with the sword foot forward, rather this is used as a demonstration that either foot can be in the forward position. The sword foot forward is just easier for the female body to work with when starting. The blow, like all of the offside blows so far, starts with the same push up and roll of the tip over and around your head. Just as in the previous shots the slight lean adds additional open area to drop the top few inches on the sword on the target leg.

Offside Head

Offside Body

Offside Leg

| Blows and Blocks

Overhead Wrap

Centerline Shot

Sweep Through Off Side Body

Attack and Defense are complementary, use each in its time.

- Sun Tzu

The top six inches of sword is often referred to as the 'sweet spot'. This is the spot that is moving the fastest when the sword is in motion. Remember that speed allows the blow to land with more power, and this is the spot that will generate the most energy. Try to aim the shots to land with this spot on the sword, you will get more power with less effort.

Offside Head

Offside Body

Offside Leg

Overhead Wrap

Centerline Shot

Sweep Through Off Side Body

> Know yourself and know your enemy, and you shall not lose a battle
>
> -Sun Tzu

> Those skilled in war can make themselves invincible but cannot cause an enemy to be vulnerable. Therefore it is said that one may know how to win, but cannot necessarily do so.
>
> - Sun Tzu

Offside Head

Offside Body

Offside Leg

Overhead Wrap

Centerline Shot

Sweep Through Off Side Body

> Conserve your energy but attack decisively, confidently and with a single mind.
>
> -Bruce Lee

Third Set: Combinations

Upper Right – Rick Rack

Middle Right – Snap and Wrap

Lower Right – Onside/Offside

Upper Left – Leg Fake

Middle Left – J shot

Lower Left – Shield Press/Offside

13. Rick Rack

This is the first of the true combinations. Combinations are the key to success in fighting, finish one shot and move on to the next without hesitation. This keeps the opponent busy, and you on the offensive. This combination starts out with a Flat Snap to the Head. In this case the opponent blocks the shot, so we move from the finish of the Snap to the Offside Head. Notice in this case that our demonstrator has moved her body to one side in an effort to 'get inside' the opponents shield.

Rick Rack

Snap and Wrap

Offside/Onside

| Blows and Blocks 147

Leg Fake

J Shot

Shield Press Offside

14. <u>Pump (Leg) Fake</u>

We've talked a little about fakes so far. Some shots start out like others and make it difficult to determine where the shot is going until the last moment. Other shots, such as combinations are actually two different shots that the opponent must block in order to survive. This is the first shot that is deliberately done as a fake. The difference here is that the first part of this shot is never intended to hit the target. To begin, move the hand up in the same manner that you did to do the over the head shot and offside shots. Instead of completing the offside shot, bring the hand back down and throw an onside shot instead.

This is not a 'basic' shot. In fact, combinations such as these sometimes take years to develop. Keep in mind that each shot of a combination is intended to be good. Don't get into the habit of expecting only the last of three shots to land. If one of the first two gets in clean, but without power, you have wasted a good victory. Practice landing each shot with precision and power. This is where the Six Part Pell drill comes in handy.

Notice that the first part of the shot is a Snap to the Head, and our model blocks the shot with just the corner of his shield. Every shield uses a different system of blocking.

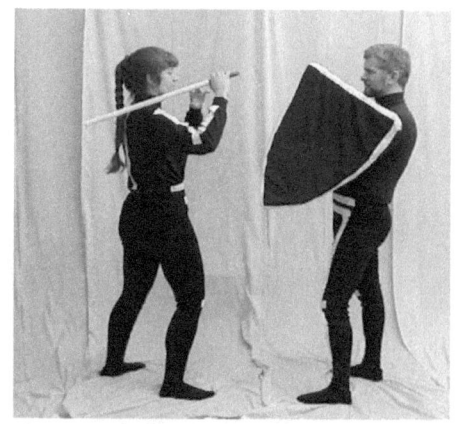
Rick Rack

Snap and Wrap

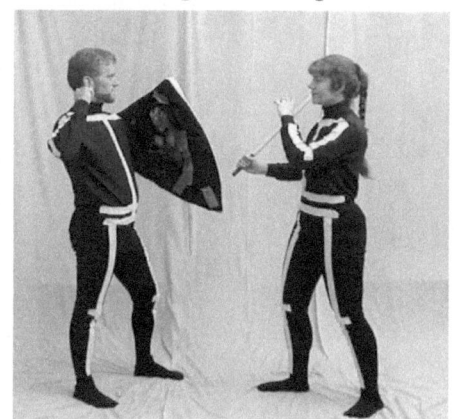
Offside/Onside

Leg Fake

J Shot

Shield Press Offside

These movements work for a number of reasons. For most fighters, at the moment a block is thrown they are blind to where the opponents stick is. The block is thrown to where they expect the stick to be. When the sword changes direction to attack the exposed side instead of the side blocked, they can not adjust in time.

The movement in a block must be scaled to the skill of the opponent. A new fighter tends to only block right before the sword hits, and often they miss. A more experienced fighter learns to recognize earlier where a blow is likely to land, and starts blocking at the first definitive motion to the target.

A heater produces a more static fight and requires minimal movement to block most shots. Rounds ask for more energy and ability to take the fight to the opponent. A Kyte helps develop movement at angles to the target. A Wankel is a very aggressive style requiring the fighter to close quickly on the opponent. Learn the basics with one style, preferably the style where you can get the most instruction. Keep in mind this may not be a Sword and Shield style at all. When I started out the best instruction available to me was with a Glaive. Whatever style you choose, stay with it long enough to learn how to attack, defend and engage in a variety of situations.

Rick Rack

Snap and Wrap

Offside/Onside

Leg Fake

J Shot

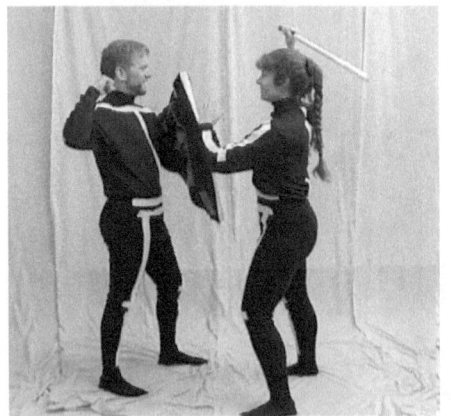
Shield Press Offside

When facing a very good fighter, a fake consists of a small twitch in one direction and striking another. One of the key points in fakes is to throw the second blow, before the opponent can recover from the first reaction.

Some people just won't bit on a fake. If they just did not see it coming, wait till they get better and it will be something you can use. If they are good enough not to fall for it, try it a few times and then turn the 'fake' into something real, and surprise them.

When you are competent, try other styles. There may be a style out there that is more suited to your temperament and nature. If your basics are strong, you will be able to translate what you know to another style quickly.

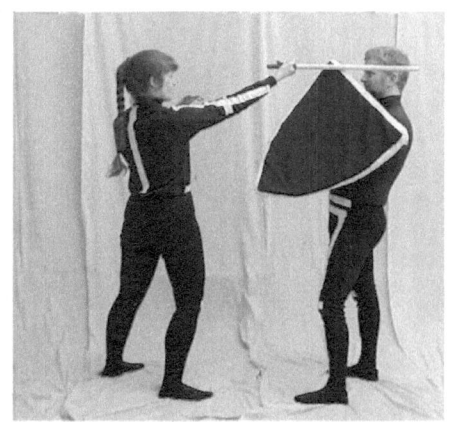

Rick Rack

Snap and Wrap

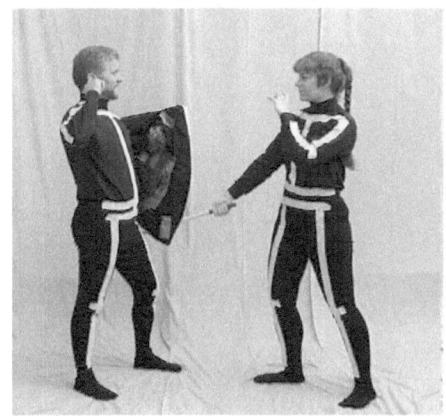

Offside/Onside

Leg Fake

J Shot

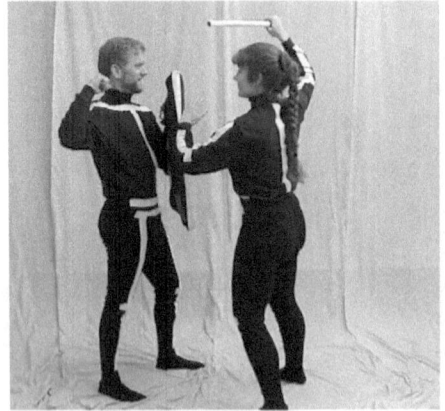

Shield Press Offside

15. J Shot

For a simple shot, the J Shot requires a lot of practice. This is sometimes called a grass cutting J or inside leg. Whatever you call this shot it must be thrown with extreme precision. The J shot is almost thrown as a Wrap shot, except that the point of the sword goes between the opponents legs and the tip comes up on the back side of the offside leg. This shot requires precision because it is far to easy to miss and strike high. It's no laughing matter when your opponent is hit straight in the cup and spends several minutes throwing up, wheezing and unable to move. Hitting a woman in the groin can do just as much damage.

16. <u>Snap to a Wrap</u>

Again this is a combination. This starts with a Snap to the Head. The sword is retrieved to nearly the starting position and then a Wrap to the Leg. Each of the elements of this shot were covered earlier. This time look at the photos and concentrate on the retrieval of the sword. Our model uses a straight back retrieval, pulling the sword into nearly the same position she started the first blow with. There are many ways to retrieve the sword. If the shot lands low try swinging it back with the tip just above the grass.

Rick Rack

Snap and Wrap

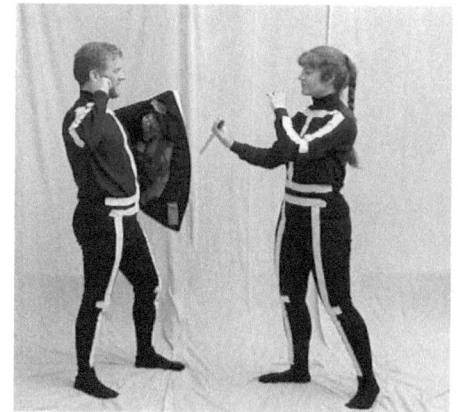

Offside/Onside

Leg Fake

J Shot

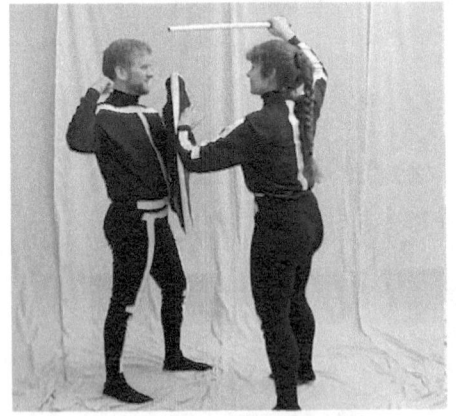
Shield Press Offside

This is one of the reasons we where armor there. It is legal, but anyone who deliberately delivers a shot to the groin is unwelcome on the field. So, don't happen to hit someone there by mistake. Practice precision.

This shot is usually done well when the person is advancing. Train your eye to see when your opponent takes a step forward with the offside leg. As soon as their foot leaves the ground, throw the shot. By the time their leg is in place to receive the blow, the blow will be ready to land and there will be no time to block. This is clearly a blow that you can not do effectively on the pell. You have to be in practice to try this.

Practice retrieving the sword in a variety of ways. Strive for a fluid motion between blow, retrieval, and the next blow. Work with the momentum of the sword. Let the direction the sword is moving in help choose where the next shot will go, you will already have much of the speed you need already in the sword. An effective visualization here is to imagine that your sword is hollow and that there is a marble in the tube. As you throw your first blow, the marble moves out to the tip of the sword. Retrieve the sword and deliver the next blow without letting the marble slide back down the tube. (You could even try this with a PVC pipe and a marble.)

Rick Rack

Snap and Wrap

Offside/Onside

Leg Fake

J Shot

Shield Press Offside

17. Shield Press move Offside

This is not so much a 'shot' as it is a sequence of moves designed to open up your opponent and gain a better attack angle. This is one of those places where the sword and shield are moving in different directions, but this time they are on the offensive together. The Sword comes up for an offside head shot. Normally the opponent would bring the corner of his shield to deflect the blow. Before they can move the shield into a blocking position though, press your shield to theirs and prevent them from blocking by trapping their shield against their body.

18. Offside/Onside

In this combination the first shot is a Snap to the Leg and then an Offside Head Shot. Notice that only the tip of the Heater is used to block the first leg shot. This is the secrete of blocking, use as little effort as possible when blocking. By moving his shield very little to block the first shot, he is in position to block a second or third shot.

Rick Rack

Snap and Wrap

Offside/Onside

| Blows and Blocks

Leg Fake

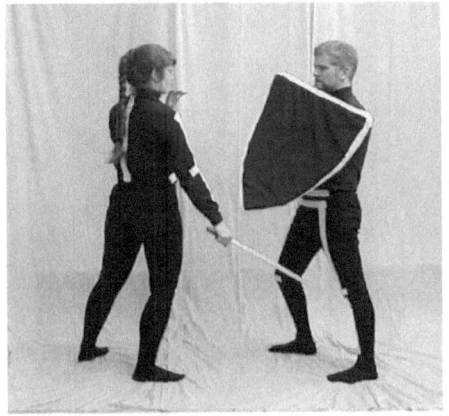
J Shot

Shield Press Offside

Be sure not to put your shield on their body and under no circumstances should you allow your shield to hit their helm. It takes more practice than you might think.

This series of pictures shows a great deal of movement on the part of the model. A significant part of fighting is about movement. You move around your opponent to gain a better advantage. You move to use their body to get in the way of their sword. You move to avoid being hit. Practice moving as well as hitting when you work on the pell.

Notice also that our model is actually ready to make a third shot. Flip through the pictures again and notice that her first shot to the legs uses her hips to drive in the power of the blow. The next shot also uses her hips, this time moving in the opposite direction, and winds her up again, ready for a third shot, where her hips will once again move counter clockwise. This takes a great deal of practice. However this technique, when done properly will allow the fighter to string several shots together and be able to "put hip" into each and every one. At first the second shot will seem a little awkward, but this is why you've been practicing the Six Part Pell. You have been practicing, haven't you?

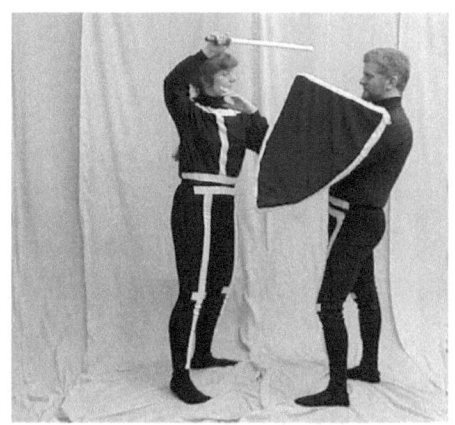

Rick Rack

Snap and Wrap

Offside/Onside

| Blows and Blocks 161

Leg Fake

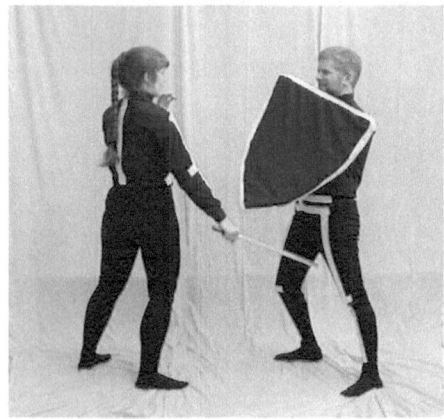

J Shot

Shield Press Offside

Only a Beginning

As you can see, we have covered many shots and a few blocks as well as a verity of techniques. Everything here is only a beginning, and only one way of doing a shot or movement. Many fighters will develop several ways to throw the same blow. Experiment. Let this be a starting point not a definitive answer for the only way to do something.

There are many more techniques to learn.

Range

We have not covered anything on Range....it is an important element. Not all fighting is done in the same range. Since this is only a primer, we will do no more than mention it.

Depending on where a trainer learned about range, they may use A, B, and C range or Long, Medium and Close range, or any other set of words. The key here is that some blows hit differently when thrown from the longer range and some need changing when they are thrown from the shorter range.

You can take the power out your opponent's shot by stepping into it (moving from Mid to short range), because the mechanic changes.

These blows are all demonstrated in the mid range, and are a fine place to start.

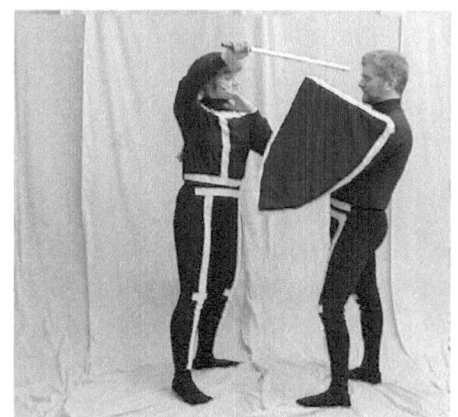
Rick Rack

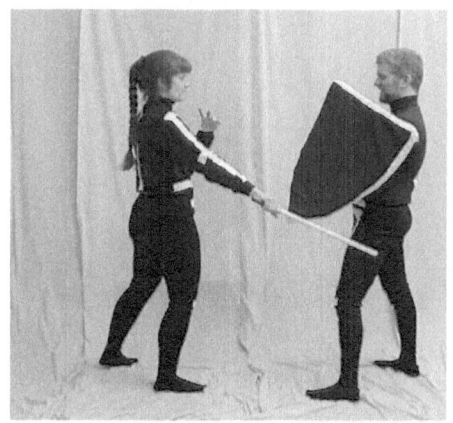
Snap and Wrap

Offside/Onside

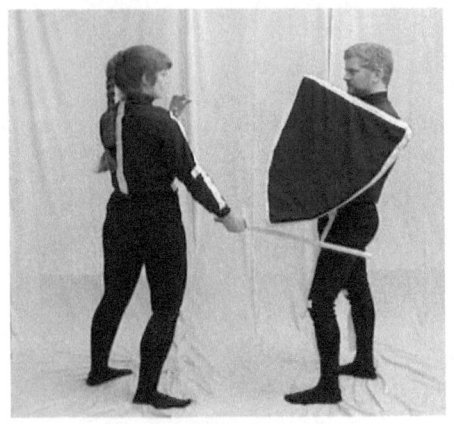
Leg Fake

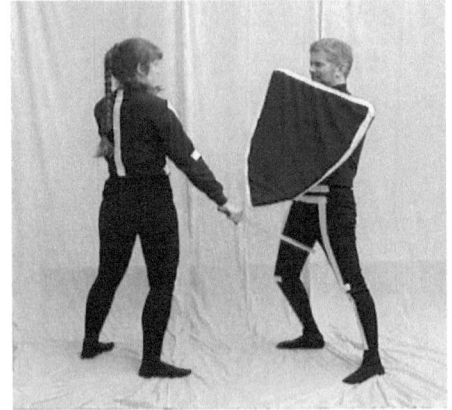
J Shot

Shield Press Offside

> If you do not push the boundaries, you will never know where thy are.
> - T. S. Elliot

> To become different from what we are, we must have some awareness of what we are.
>
> -Bruce Lee

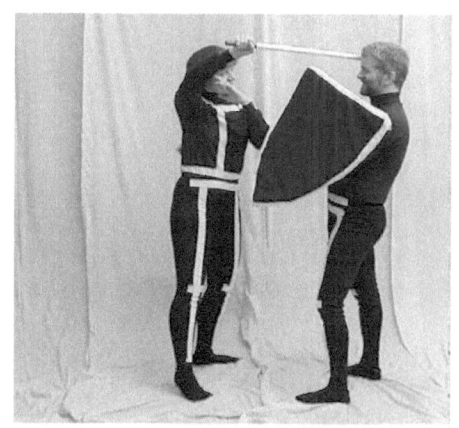
Rick Rack

Snap and Wrap

Offside/Onside

| Blows and Blocks

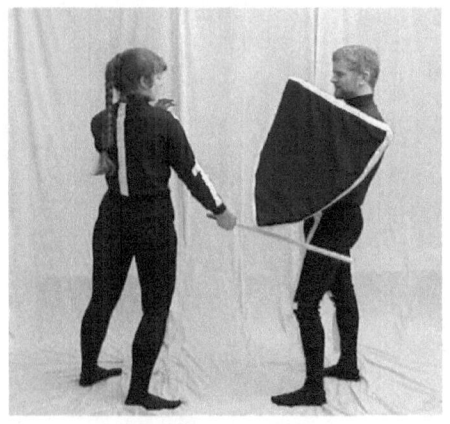
Leg Fake

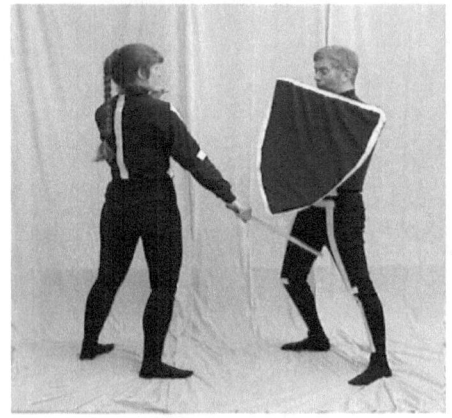
J Shot

Shield Press Offside

Action which is undertaken in the company of associates, family, friends, as well as expert and thoughtful persons is considered to be the best.

-The Way of Kings, 4000 BC

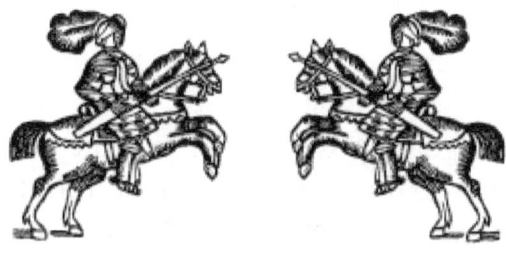

Practice drills on your own

Drills that you do on your own are great practice. So, you can't get to fighter practice every night, or maybe it's raining or well, any number of reasons to be working on your own. There are several drills you can do to hone your skill and reflexes. Here are a few:

1. The six part pell: This is an excellent pell practice, shown to me by Duke Jade of Starfall [West Kingdom/SCA. The drill, when done consistently, will develop the ability to move from one target to the next in a fluid motion. This ability is the building block of all combinations. There are those who will throw 12-15 blows in a single combination, each one an effective kill if it lands. The opponent is usually so busy blocking that there is no time to attack. If they can't attack, they can't win.

First, mentally divide the pell into 6 zones. The lower right ["right leg"] being 1, the middle right ["right body"] being 2, the upper right ["right head"] being 3, the upper left ["left head"] being 4, the middle left ["left body"] being 5, and the lower left ["left leg"] being 6. (see Diagram 1)

Stand in the en guard position and face the pell. Start with point 1 as the primary location. Deliver a shot to 1 and then again to 1. Next 1 and then 2. Next, 1 and 3. Then 1 and 4, 1 and 5, 1 and 6. That is the completion of part one of the exercise.

From here, the drill starts again, but with 2 being the primary location, with the secondary shot moving around the pell to all locations [1-6] Hit 2 and 1, 2 and 2, 2 and 3, 2 and 4 and so on. Next, 3 is the primary, and the secondary moves through 1-6 as normal. This practice continues around the pell until all locations have been "primaries." [If you wish, you can start at 6 and move in the other direction....]

When the basic idea is understood, you can work on the way shots are delivered. Do not limit yourself to straight snaps or backhands, but include wraps, "punches", quick pull and returns, long arcs, etc. Use the idea behind this drill to polish your transition from one shot to the next, to make it fluid and elegant. Ultimately, you can include lunges, steps, and other body movement into this drill. This may seem to be a bit arduous, but it will train you to work your body and weapon motion so that you can deliver a killing blow from any other location where a previous shot was thrown. It will also help your eye~hand coordination. This will help in your ability to get that sword to a target that has just opened, in an expedient or subtle manner.

If using a polearm, you may wish to include the butt spike [if any] in the process. This drill will also help you to maintain proper degrees of arc allowed with pole weapons. If using the point, you will benefit from this practice as well. Your precision of attack, recovery, parry [and arm muscles!] will all show definite improvement. When you think your good, divide the pell into 12 targets, 6 on the front, six on the back.

(Diagram 1)

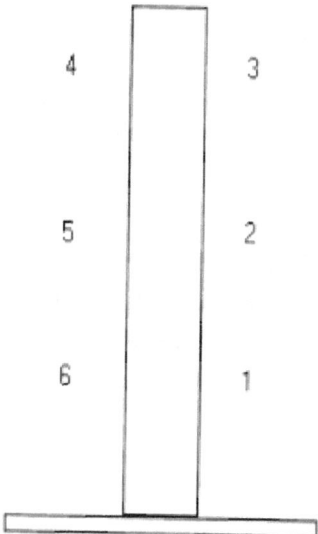

2. Tennis Ball Target: This drill requires a pell of a different kind, shown to me by Countess Mari Greensleeves. This pell is made of an S hook at the top, which you can clip into another S-hook that you put in the ceiling someplace. The S-hook is attached to a cord and the cord to a sand filled tennis ball. A cord comes out the other end of the ball and goes to a second sand filled tennis ball, about head level. (See Diagram 2)

Tap the lower tennis ball with a dowel or practice stick. The ball will move in unpredictable arcs and swings. Continue to throw blows to tap it as it is in motion. The drill will develop skill at hitting a moving target and predicting where the target will be next. This eye hand coordination is vital in developing precision and target selection.

This drill develops the hand, eye, stick and distance coordination. It is important to know where the end of the stick is in order to place the shots on the "sweet spot" of the stick.

Diagram 2

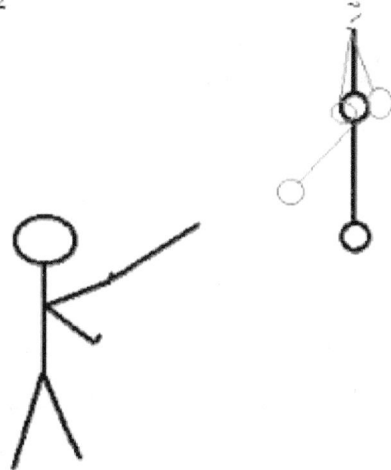

2. **Put a Stick in your Hand.** Every day. Get a broomstick the length of your sword, a thick dowel or a piece of rattan. Put it in your hand every day for an hour. Practice hitting things. Not hard, with precision. I don't recommend practicing on the china, but try an old wicker chair or a ladder. Practice hitting the inside of one of the holes on the ladder without hitting the side. Practice touching objects at full distance to develop a sense of where the end of the sword is. Practice touching objects as you move past them. Do this when you walk the dog, on your way to the park, between classes at school, when you walk to lunch and back. Work at it, you can find an hour of your day where this simple exercise can be worked in.

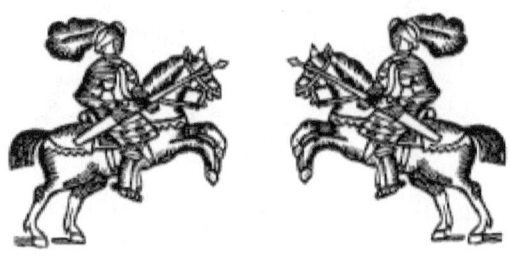

Practice Drills with a Partner

Many trainers say they don't know any training drills, and many women don't feel they learn anything from fighting all out. Here are a few training drills to do with a partner that develop various aspects of fighting.

1. What's Next?: This drill is based on the principle that all parts of the body can not be covered all the time. If the opponent moves the shield to cover his head, he exposes his leg. If a leg wrap is blocked, the opposite body opens up. In this drill the trainer takes the shield and holds a target open for the student to reach for the shot. Don't hit hard or even at speed, this is a drill and the object is to see openings, not dent the trainer.

Once the shot has started, in slow motion, the trainer moves to block. When the trainer blocks the shot, something else opened up. The trainer freezes in the new block position and allows the student to see and decide what target is now available. As the student takes the shot, the trainer blocks again, opening another target.

At first this drill will take several seconds between shots and may require the trainer to point out what is open. As the student practices the openings will become more clear and the drill will become faster. This is an extension of the first solo exercise, from any location you will learn to see and deliver a blow to another location.

2. Twenty and Three: Here the student gets to take twenty shots either in combinations or singly. The trainer has only three to use. It's more fair than it sounds. All to often the emphasis in on attack and the defense falls away. The student has twenty shots to make, think about and take. The trainer must block them. The student, however can not be so absorbed in the attack that they forget to defend. The trainer has three shots, if the student ignores their defense the trainer will score a hit. Count your score at the end of the drill. (I'll give you a hint, my score was 0-3 for a looooong time.)

3. Half Speed: This drill is exactly what it says, but is not as easy as it sounds. Both student and teacher are in full armor and stand as if to fight. Each moves as if they were in molasses and only moving at half speed. Imagine everything moving in slow motion. It is absolutely forbidden to speed up in order to prevent from being tagged. Since you are moving very slow, there is no pain in being touched. The drill is about control and seeing openings and movement in fluid consistency. Move from one shot to the next, one block to the next, never speeding up, but looking for what is open on you and what is open on the opponent.

Try not to get into a block – hit –block – hit pattern. This has a tendency to develop this pattern when fighting and you will wait for the person to hit back before starting the next shot. Try not to flail uncontrollably at the opponent, select your targets and go for what is open.

When done properly, this is a fluid dance. Do your best to maintain this as only half speed. This is an excellent warm up drill and many a Duke still use it before starting an all out fight at practice.

As the student progresses, move to three-quarters speed. Many of the movements are the same, but the increased speed will require a little more muscle control and momentum no longer behaves the same. Always make an agreement to move from half to three-quarters, don't just creep up there. Because the dynamics are different between these two speeds it is important to agree to which speed you are at. This drill develops control, and fluidity.

It is much harder however to avoid creeping from three-quarters to full speed. Movement and momentum are very similar at three-quarters and full and moving from one to the other is often done without conscious thought. At three-quarters speed the student will progress to full speed as they are ready.

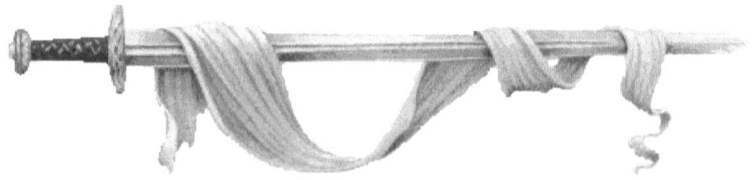

VII. Promise

A few years back I met a woman who would become a friend in time. She and I had fought for a number of years and we were each just starting to make our way in the uncertain field of fighting. She had written a short paper as a means of venting the frustration that she felt, and encouraging others. While we had never spoken of our trials to each other, she asked me to read the paper. In some measure, I saw myself in her words and discovered that others felt the same frustrations I felt. The more I talked to others, the more I realized that the trials are nearly universal. Her writing provided a healthy dose of humor and with her permission I have included it here in its entirety. It should be noted that since the original writing of this book Mari, now Duchess Mari, has also been knighted.

My Lady Doth Carry a Big Stick

Duchess Mari aka Mari Asonte, OL, OP, KSCA

I decided I wanted to fight. Easy enough, but I also decided I didn't want to feel like a complete idiot at fighter practice. This had a simple solution; learn the basics in the privacy of my own backyard. Since I have the luxury of having my own personal Duke-in-residence and a pell, training began.

There's so much to learn! First, stand like this; face the pell at a forty five degree angle, bend your knees, keep your back straight, head forward, arm back. Great! Now what? Now let's hand you a stick. Straight snap – Hand goes out guiding your hilt straight towards the target, close your hand, bend the wrist, swing the sword around and HIT! And, <u>while</u> you're doing that, keep your weight equally distributed between both feet, push forward with your sword-side hip to add power to the move and VOILA! Except keep your knees bent, don't raise the heel of that back foot, get your hand up higher – the proper hand angle is essential to the effectiveness of this blow!

Aaarrrrgh! And that's just one blow. The choice at this point is to either practice until you get it or throw the sword down and stomp on it until you feel better. Be careful. Swords roll.

You Continue. Finally there are three or four blows you can do if your life depends on it. Congratulate yourself heartily, because he's going to hand you a shield. Everything you just learned changes. Oh no, not a lot, just enough to confuse the issue, your balance is a little different, there's a board where your sword wants to be – subtle things.

Our next step is boffer swords. You have a shield, fencing mask and boffer. He has shield, helmet and white belt. Hardly seems fair.

Okay, hit him – just like you do the pell. No problem, except I don't recall the pell blocking quite so well. What do you mean he didn't move the shield? Sigh, hand up . . . . angle remember, angle.

And then he hits you back. Maybe he's a generous Duke and tells you how to hold the shield and the principals of blocking before he hits you. Then again, maybe he doesn't. By the time you block a dozen blows, excuse me, by the time you try to block a dozen blows, your arm is ready to fall off. Isn't this fun? Call a truce, find a hot tub and eat chocolate, you'll feel much better.

Finding a hot tub isn't overly important at this point in the game, but it's a good time to start looking. By the time you're done with your first full day of war you'll want to have guaranteed access to one all taken care of.

You go out and play boffers again. He tells you, "Don't aim at my shield." Does he think you're an idiot? If you aimed at his shield you'd never hit him. Then again, he may have something there. He blocks your first four blows – and never moves his shield. You miss his first four blows – and never move your shield. And this is slow work.

Now for your armor. Whether you make, beg, borrow or steal your armor be prepared to be very patient with it. You strap it, you pad it, you put it on for the first time piece by piece. . . and it feels so AWKWARD! You clunk around, it doesn't feel right, it binds here, pinches there, chaffs around here . . .sigh. Throw it in a pile and burn it. Seems like a rational decision, doesn't it?

Well, metal doesn't burn so well, so call a truce, find a hot tub and eat chocolate.

Better? Back to the armor.

Slowly it comes together and the bugs get knocked out of it (lice, fleas, spiders). It is important that your armor is reasonably comfortable if you are serious about continuing to fight. If you dread getting into it, you won't. I've found through trial and error that open-faced helms are wonderful. Oxygen comes in, carbon dioxide goes out . . . what a concept!

So now you have armor (or some rough resemblance thereof). Dukey takes you out, you both suit up (ever notice how natural he looks in his armor, how well he moves, how unencumbered he seems? It's done with mirrors). You feel as graceful as a small tank, your body moves in slow motion, your sword arm.. . oh traitorous sword arm. . . weighs a ton. Get your hand up . . angle remember. But you can't get it past shoulder height. Aaaarrrgh!

The weeks go by. Block, block, whack, whack. Your shield is beginning to catch blows, your sword occasionally rings true against his helm (you suspect a soft spot in his Grace's sadistic nature). As you fight you begin to notice a certain inability to accomplish multiple functions. You can block OR you can hit. If you think about hitting, your shield becomes inert. If you concentrate on blocking, your sword sits on your shoulder with no inclination to perform all the brilliant blows you have taught it. And while you overcome this slight inconvenience, you discover that your hip has forgotten to move with the blow and your feet are dancing the Karabushka while the rest of you is trying to Bransel. Truce, hot tub, chocolate.

Finally you feel prepared to show your armored self at fighter practice. Remember to go through <u>all</u> your armor and miscellaneous equipment and make sure it's all there and it all works. Nothing quite so embarrassing as not having your helm at your first practice when <u>everyone</u> is expecting you to be out there. And they will be, trust me, unless you have kept this a deep dark secret. If that's the case then surprise them, but you'll still need all your gear.

You suit up, the armor is starting to feel good, put your hat on and go arrange your first dance. Now, these people aren't strangers, they're friends – friends who just happen to want to hit you repeatedly with large sticks. Go out, have fun.

At fighter practice you discover a wonderful thing, there are some people who don't care if they look like idiots at fighter practice and they go out with no training. You can kill them. More frequently than they can kill you. O frabjous day! Callooh! Callay! You chortle in your joy.

Warning: These people are in the minority.

However, the better you are the more people there will be who you can kill. It's a nice theory. I learned it from my Duke.

As you fight more and more frequently the opportunities for The Deterrent increase. What is The Deterrent? Pain. Pure and simple. It may have happened the first time you put on armor, it may have happened the second time, or the fifth or the tenth. But it happens t all of us eventually. Sometimes it begins simply enough; you're on your knees, some brute is pummelling at your helm, your shield is catching the blows and raising higher and higher. Suddenly your shield has become a table, you're serving up an order of ribs and he's doing the carving. Yowza! I hope you cot some pads on those ribs sweetheart or they'll be colorchrome by morning.

Or maybe you did it the easy way and let your Duke take a mace out against you. Oh ow!

This brings us to bruises. Purple, blue, black, red, green, yellow. Lovely, eh? And they hurt. Not always, but frequently enough. And the worst ones are the ones with no color at all. The hurt like hell and leave no evidence of your agony.

So be aware that when you are dressing in your skimpy bikini, the stares you receive are not all in admiration of your lovely curves and muscles, some are reserved for the incredible coloring below your left ass cheek.

And what does all the practice lead to? Tournament and War! The glory of the crowds, pennants waving, heralds shouting – and the joys of battle. Hazza!

So you want to be Queen? Find somebody to agree to let you fight for them and bear their favor proudly as you go to meet the foe in their honor. Have you played consort in the past? Interesting switch, isn't it?

At invocation you stand there before Their Majesties (or Highnesses, as the case may be) looking at this long line of white belted folks.[1] Who should you challenge to slaughter you first round? At this point you have the option of picking someone you might have a chance of killing, say that up-and-coming unbelt

Their Majesties made a knight-for-a-day, or you can pick the biggest, baddest contender out there. The latter has a couple of advantages. If you lose, you don't have to feel too badly – this guy is going to kill everybody or almost everybody he fights. And if you win – if you WIN you have scored the greatest coup imaginable to a new stick-Jane.

This brings us to the first tourney win. Don't feel bad if you go out in the second round you first few tournaments. You're in good company, twenty-five percent of the folks out there are not going to hear their name in the third round. The first to die, the first to shower. Of course, the gods may smile on you, and you may kill all who oppose you your first tournament - not bloody likely. But you may kill one. Third round, here you come! Tell everyone. You have stood victorious on the tourney field, you foe slain at your feet. There is no need to relate your amazement as you saw them fall, it is enough that they have fallen. You have years in which to dissect every fight and analyze every move. Leave this one alone to stand in glory. All too soon you also shall be numbered among the fallen.

But that's not the only way to die. There's war. Wars are designed to allow the average green pike-fodder (that's you and me, Babe) to practice their dying a multitude of times in a multitude of ways. Resurrection wars allow you to do this rapidly. Oh, what fun.

Most of us learn basic one-on-one fighting at practice. Occasionally we have melees (mini wars with different rules). Nothing but war prepares you for war. In day to day fighting, most folks carry a shield and a sword. There are odd folks out there, but this is what we see the most of. Wars are an excuse to drag every weirdo can-opener out of the garage. You got the somewhat normal stuff; pikes, axes, great axes, maces, great swords, mauls, glaves, javelins and arrows. Then there's the hybrid stuff that is bred during the long winter season when the axe and the glave are left alone for too long in the dark together.

The trouble with wars is that similar stimuli do not hold equal importance. The pike nine feet away may very well be far more dangerous to your well being than the glave four feet away. Or the man with the broadsword in front of you is not near as lethal as the man directly to his left. Pay attention to all of it, prioritization comes with experience. Mostly bad experience.

Remember that hot tub? This is the time for it. You take off your armor at the end of a long hard day of fighting, count your bruises and you realize that your entire body hurts. Your arms hurt, your shoulders hurt, your legs hurt, your head hurts, all the muscles throughout your back are in agony. And you stink, you lord won't even hug you. It's definitely hot tub time.

Enjoy the warmth of the water bubbling about you. Enjoy the company of your comrades-at-arms as you exchange no-shit-there-I-was stories. You are a warrior. As time passes more of the mysteries of the sword will be revealed to you. You will learn that the more you know, the more there is to know. Someday in the hazy future perhaps you too will win the throne by your own hand, or join the ranks of the knight. Best of luck to you sister. Enjoy your chocolate.

♦ In the Kingdom of the West the knights are set to one side and top rank non-knights are crossed over to the knight's side to even up the lines. The unbelted side, one by one, then choose their first fight of the list.

The author of this piece was knighted in the Kingdom of the West in 2010.

I've met and re-met Sir Maythen a number of times in the last several years. While I can not claim to be close, I can say that we have had some of the most involved and intriguing conversations and I count her among friends. If you choose to cross wits or swords with the women, be prepared for an excellent time, she will never fail you there. I asked if she would share a moment of her learning with others, so that they could gain from her experience. She may have had specific people in mind when she wrote this, but it could easily be any Kingdom any Duke, any Knight, and any Little Girl.

The Magic Sword

By Dana Kramer-Rolls, a.k.a. Viscountes Sir Maythen Gervaise (of Elfhaven), Duchess Hoghton

Once upon a time… don't all good stories begin this way… once upon a time there was a Girl, a dreamer, who wanted to do everything. She did not want to be a princess, or a cheerleader, or a movie star. She wanted to be a king, a quarterback, a director. She didn't want to be a helper. She wanted to be a leader. She was good in the theater and school, but, that was just because she was a good dreamer. So what she dreamed became real for people, people who mostly dreamed in black and white. Her dreams gave them color. And they liked that. And she liked that. But people moved on, and she dreamed mostly by herself.

She lived in a secret world, a world of Arthur and Robin Hood, of castles and greenwood, and also in a world of Buck Rogers and Flash Gordon and John Carter of Mars. There were no Dragon Riders back then or SCA or SF conventions. There was magic in her home, but it was secret. There was no pagan community, no Early Music society. There was practically nothing that helped make the dreams real.

When she studied fencing as a child the fencing master (a rather famous old coot) asked her what she wanted to study and she had said "Broadsword" and he laughed at her and she studied foil. She made fairy clothes out of leaves and read English books (they seemed to know Things) and played dress up with old curtains and grew to love science as well as fantasy for the wonder of the night sky and the magic in the fields and woods. But there was no place for a little girl like that, or if there was, she didn't know about it. Worse, she thought she was the only one in the world like her. And she was sad.

She grew up and did many things, but always she dreamed. And always, even after there were others who dreamed the same dream, she somehow felt she was alone. Some door wouldn't open, some magic spell hadn't been said, to set her free.

The SCA was wonderful and terrible. It was creative and exciting and full of people who had been outsiders, who had never made the team in school or were the last to be picked in the schoolyard games, and people who dreamed. It was indeed a society with households and politics and friends and even enemies. But everything and everybody was larger than life. The SCA was still pretty small, back then, and new, and everybody knew everybody more or less. And one could still remember the names of all the Kings of the West, and all the wars, and all the really good jests that happened at court, and it could truly be said it was a world of Heroes. Even the great feuds between great households were epic. It was like living in the legends and sagas. It was dreaming come to life. And the Girl Now a Woman, was hopeful.

Fighting was the best. Fighting was everything. The Girl Now a Woman had already learned to bake and brew and sew and make music in her other life. She had already begun to build a magic cottage in her home out of her dreams. The reality of divorce and a vicious custody battle couldn't kill that. But the fighting… that was what she always dreamed of. Honor. Fealty. Courage. Those things had painted the color in her dreams. Now they were coming into life.

The Trolls (that was not their real name, but this is a fairy tale) were a noble band of friends who were not trolls at all. In fact they were so sensible that they saw the dangers in letting one's dreams go to one's head. Not that they didn't dream. Oh, boy, could they dream. But they really didn't like some Duke Famous or Sir Wonderful taking his dream and making it the Official Dream and anybody who didn't dream that way was "The most unchivalrous person I ever met." Not that Duke F. or Sir W. weren't noble and fine men, but they got a little uppity about their success, which was usually not their fault but the good genes they got from their mommy and daddy.

So the Trolls decided to do something about it. They started a training school, oh, not one of those "I am sensei and you will obey" schools. There were already enough of those. But one where just plain folks who dreamed could come and learn…and TEACH! That's right, teach, from the beginning, because the Trolls believed we were all smart and had something to offer. And the best thing the Trolls did was they gathered around them a lot of Girls, who were Now Women, because they didn't think that women were being treated fairly. How about that!

The Girl Now a Woman was not a real Troll. She was engaged to a Duke, not Duke Famous, but Duke Almost-as-Famous who didn't much care for "I am sensei and you will obey" schools. So she and her knight, the Duke, tagged along with the Trolls. It was wonderful. First slow warm-ups. Then each practice began with some venerable old drills. Stand there and hold your shield up for one or two minutes (that is a Long Time), and try not to get hit. Just to keep it honest, the hit-ee got three blows on the hitter, and if you got one in you got it back. Stuff like that. Sometimes you couldn't move from a given square and you had to fight it out. Sometimes there were off-handed drills and lost-your-shield one handed drills. Whatever anybody could think of that would help.

And then there was a round robin. Everybody got to fight everybody. When the group on any given night was small and it was winter with tourney season far away, everybody would watch one person take on each fighter in turn and then offer criticism. Yes, everybody was a critic! Everybody from Sir Trolls 1 and 2 and Duke Almost-As-Famous to Ms. Newbee. Because the Trolls believed everybody was smart enough to know something worth sharing. And it was good practice to learn how to watch a fight critically. If there was extra energy, the practice would end with a few melees, or a meat-grinder (hold the field until you get killed or fall down with exhaustion), or both.

Trolls weren't much on squires, because being a squire was neat but it had become something of indentured servitude and a way to get a swelled head. And Not Getting a Swelled Head is what this was all about. That and having some good women fighters to challenge those knights who wouldn't fight a woman because it wasn't chivalrous. Those knights never said whom it wasn't chivalrous for. It didn't do much for the chivalry of the woman challenging. The Trolls always suspected that it wasn't respect for women but the lack of it. So at practice there wasn't much patience with bowing and scraping. Everybody had a name, mundane usually unless the SCA name had really stuck, and that's what they got called.

Sometimes, in the Spring when the practice moved to a lovely private college and it was all green and trees and birds singing, and it didn't get dark until late, the Trolls held a round robin tourney at every practice after the warm-up drills. And at the end the tally would be read. And it was wonderful. Sir Troll 1 or 2 didn't always win, although they always fought. Sometimes someone who hadn't been fighting long or someone who was a complete surprise would up and win.

But our hero, the Girl Now A Woman, couldn't kill anybody. She had gone out in tourney after tourney, even Crown Tourney, practice after practice, and somehow she would always lose. Her technique was good. She was brave. She was fierce. But she couldn't win. And giving them a good run for their money was not a happy thing. And here it was worse, against other women and men who were fair. What was wrong? Why was she always at the bottom of the list when the tally of the round robin came in?

One evening at the lovely college the frustration bubbled over. She couldn't hold it in anymore, she couldn't pretend with nice words about how that was a good fight or how much better she was getting. She quit. She burst into tears and she quit. She told her Duke and lover that she just couldn't go on. Then she got into her helm to finish the round robin, which had already begun, promising herself to give away her armor when it was over. She was crying all the time she fought, the tears oozing down her face. She reached back to throw yet another blow which wouldn't land or wouldn't count or wouldn't something and she felt someone grab her arm.

Before she could look back, she felt her sword being taken away, and another put in her hand. It was her Duke's favorite tourney sword, a big, heavy old clunker with a cross hilt that was too short and off balance by everybody else's rights. And the fight resumed as seamlessly as it had stopped. And she hit her opponent. And her opponent fell to the ground. And the Girl Now a Woman looked down at her feet at her companion lying there, stunned, and then looked up to the field of fighters grinding away at their round robin list and cried out "Next!" She killed five in a row, and pretty soon was the undoubted champion of the practice, or at least toe to toe with all the rest of the trainees and even the Troll Knights.

What had happened? What made it different? Was it just that her Duke loved her and didn't want her to give up? Was it that the sword carried the magic of a Duke of the West? In some part yes, but not entirely. If that were so then it wouldn't have been her victory. She would have just been another damsel saved by a guy, not an equal and companion. And that is what she wanted. What had happened? The door had opened, the magic had happened.

Somehow in that moment and with that sword, his love and faith in her, and her dreams and her desire and maybe a stray Valkyrie or two had met and merged and the universe changed forever, at least for the Woman who now held the field. She felt taller (a feat for one only five feet tall), and stronger, and she held her head in a way she had never done before. And the magic didn't fail. It was there, and there for good. All the fencing masters who laughed and the school kids who mocked and "being the only one" and the "girls don't do those things" swept away. And she was never the same, never broken, never incomplete, again. And that was a wonderful thing. And if they didn't all live happily ever after, they made a good run at it, and they lived good and contented loves for a long, long time. Oh, and by the way, the Girl got to be a Princess after all, all by herself!

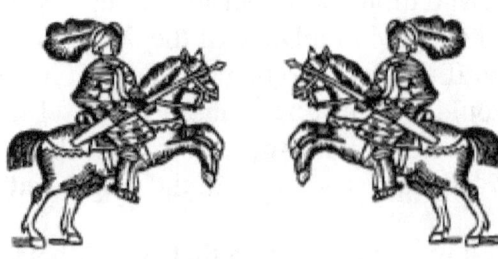

It seems a little odd, writing a short story for encouragement after writing the whole book, but this is a place for personal history, not just lessons, a glimpse into the author if you will. You can do this.

The Time of My Life

By Tobi Beck aka Duchess Elina of Beckenham, OL,OR, OP

I started fighting when I was 18. My brother fought. My boyfriend fought. My friends fought. Why shouldn't I fight? There were all sorts of people to help. People to show me how to make armor, people to teach me.

So, I was a little oblivious to the not so subtle pressure that said I should not fight. I wanted to fight, but it was so hard to go to practice. Once I was there, it was so hard to put on armor. Once the armor was on, it was so hard to get into a fight. My feet were in cement every step of the way. It just did not make sense. I really wanted to fight.

I was fortunate enough to fall into a household that made fighting a game that everyone could play. The head of the House agreed to teach me, but his way. I wanted to learn Florentine. He wanted me to be useful to the unit and taught me Glaive instead. I wanted to fight in the main body. He wanted me to learn how to move in a strike team.

When I didn't fight we played games. Games like "Helm Ball". Take your favorite weapon, an empty gallon milk jug and volleyball net. Play volleyball, without your hands, only your weapons. Your skill in the game is directly proportional to your skill as a fighter. Trust me on this. Five squires on one side and one Duke on the other. We only won when we rushed him and pinned him to the ground pummeling him with the milk jug.

It took a while to actually engage in a fight. It's easy to hide in a group and die quickly, no one notices that you really didn't exactly fight back. A full quarter of the clan was female. When we fought in wars we learned to put paint on our faces to disguise our gender. More of my blows were called and I got called 'my lord' a great deal. The wars were fun, the camaraderie great. I was well respected and needed by the clan. But still, it was hard to practice, harder still to fight one on one. I fought because my knight wanted me too. I fought for the group.

It's not that I could not fight one on one. You have to fight one on one in order to authorize. I just didn't want to. I fought in a few tournaments. I won a couple. I began to like using a Glaive, even if it wasn't my first choice. Once I was deemed useful in this style, I began to teach it to others in the clan. The Duke started to teach me Florentine. I, of course, moved away. Life comes first.

I eventually began to learn Sword and Shield from my husband. He swears he never moved his shield when we started. When he did move his shield so I would hit him, I apologized. I didn't want to hit my love. What? How could I do that? I mean that I was out here swinging a stick at him, wasn't I? Of course I meant to hit him. I was SO confused. I learned Sword and Shield because I wanted to be a knight. Every knight needs to know how to use them, or so they believe where I live. Besides fighting a new form never hurts if you know your basics already.

I still dragged myself to practice. I still waited until well into the evening before putting on my armor. I may have only fought one fight, and then sit out or talk to others for the rest of the practice. But I still wanted to be a knight. So I fought. Every night after practice it hurt. My back would ache. My knee would swell. Fighting hurt. Not from being hit, it hurt from what I was doing to my body in order to fight. But I still wanted to be a knight. Everyone else said this was fun, and I was trying to have fun, but it was so hard to force myself to fight.

Night after night I would ask myself, "Self, why won't you fight?" In the quiet of the night I learned to listen to the little voice inside *"Because, girls don't fight."* "Why do you feel bad when you beat someone?" *"Because girls aren't suppose to win games they play with boys."* "Why do you cry?" *"Because girls have done something wrong when they are hit, you should be ashamed."*

Night after night I questioned the little voice. I followed the words of Sun-Tzu, "Know the enemy, and know yourself, and you will be victorious." I learn about the enemy, the one I called the Lizard Brain. I then started to talk to others and ask them about their little voice. I sought out the sociologists to learn where it came from. And I sought out the physiologists to learn it's methods. I learned how the wily creature acted. I learned how to beat it.

Day after day I would talk to doctors and physical therapists. I learned about the differences between a man's body and a woman's. I experimented with the body I own, and I began to find a better way. Many, many more experienced fighters sought to correct me and turn me back to the tried and true path of proper fighting. But I learned, instead, to find a new road, one for my body, one for my mind. Each of us takes our own road to mastery. Mine was just unmarked.

I've heard all the arguments the Lizard Brain has put forward, and I've learned how to ignore them. I have a roll of duct tape handy and I've learned to wrap it around its snout to shut it up. I learned to fight in a form that works with my body, so that it does not hurt to play. I no longer fight just to be a knight, or because my unit depends on me, or because it's expected. I fight for all those reasons now, but mostly because I want to. I've learned to fight, because it's fun. I'm in armor every chance I get and at every practice I can go to. I hop in armor as soon as I can and won't get out until I have too. Once I understood where my path was I began to have the time of my life.

But then I realized other people were in the place I was before, and since I had found a path, how could I do anything else but help others find it as well? Adventures are more fun when there is company.

Use this book as a signpost. A path is there, waiting for you. You can do this. Come join me.

About the Author

Tobi Beck was born in Silver Spring, Maryland. She graduated from the University of South Florida in 1991 with a BA in Communications, and a Commission in the United States Army. She holds a PhD in Humanities and a Juris Doctorate.

Tobi joined the SCA in 1980 and began fighting in 1984. She served in the Active Duty Army as an Officer in the Military Police Corps where she was stationed at Ft. McClullean, AL, Ft. Ord, CA, and Ft. Lewis, WA. She saw tours of duty in Guantanamo Bay, Haiti and Somalia and performed various MP operations throughout the continental US. While in the military she traveled to places the SCA has never been, and from one Kingdom to another. Her experience fighting in the SCA, as well as in the military, provided the insight and education to begin a comparison between men and women – from the physical to the physiological. Her knowledge of combat proved that women could be as effective as their male counterparts, but that they learned and approached problems differently. She learned from this to teach people based on their strengths. Tobi began formally teaching this approach and form of fighting in 1996 and travels throughout the Known World lecturing. Tobi currently works as a Technology Manager in Indianapolis, IN and lives with her husband - Steve, son - Ethan, two dogs and a cat raised by a Doberman.

www.ingramcontent.com/pod-product-compliance
Lightning Source LLC
Chambersburg PA
CBHW020939180426
43194CB00038B/406